The OFFICIAL
HIGHWAY
CODE

We're turning over a new leaf.

WORLD
LAND
TRUST™
www.carbonbalancedprint.com
CBP2223

MIX
Paper | Supporting
responsible forestry
FSC® C002151
www.fsc.org

Contents

Introduction

This Highway Code applies to England, Scotland and Wales. *The Highway Code* is essential reading for everyone.

The aim of *The Highway Code* is to promote safety on the road, whilst also supporting a healthy, sustainable and efficient transport system.

Many of the rules in the Code are legal requirements, and if you disobey these rules you are committing a criminal offence. You may be fined, given penalty points on your licence or be disqualified from driving. In the most serious cases you may be sent to prison. Such rules are identified by the use of the words '**MUST/MUST NOT**'. In addition, the rule includes an abbreviated reference to the legislation which creates the offence. An explanation of the abbreviations is in Annex 4.

Although failure to comply with the other rules of the Code will not, in itself, cause a person to be prosecuted, *The Highway Code* may be used in evidence in any court proceedings under the Traffic Acts (see Annex 4) to establish liability. This includes rules which use advisory wording such as 'should/should not' or 'do/do not'.

Knowing and applying the rules contained in *The Highway Code* could significantly reduce road casualties. Cutting the number of deaths and injuries that occur on our roads every day is a responsibility we all share. *The Highway Code* can help us discharge that responsibility. Further information on driving/riding techniques can be found in *The Official DVSA Guide to Driving – the essential skills* and *The Official DVSA Guide to Riding – the essential skills*.

Self-driving vehicles

By 'self-driving vehicles', we mean those listed as automated vehicles by the Secretary of State for Transport under the Automated and Electric Vehicles Act 2018. To check if your vehicle is self-driving, visit www.gov.uk/guidance/self-driving-vehicles-listed-for-use-in-great-britain

These vehicles are capable of safely driving themselves when the self-driving function is correctly turned on and the driver follows the manufacturer's instructions. While the vehicle is driving itself, you do not need to monitor it.

Self-driving vehicles differ from vehicles that are fitted only with assisted driving features (like cruise control and lane-keeping assistance). Assisted driving features can do some of the driving, but the driver still needs to be responsible for driving at all times. If you are driving a vehicle using only its assisted driving features, Rule 150 applies.

A self-driving vehicle's ability to drive itself may be limited to certain situations or parts of a journey. Things like the type of road, time of day, weather, location and speed may affect this. You should follow the manufacturer's instructions about when and how to use the self-driving function safely.

While a self-driving vehicle is driving itself in a valid situation, you are not responsible for how it drives. You may turn your attention away from the road and you may also view content through the vehicle's built-in infotainment apparatus, if available.

But you **MUST** still follow all relevant laws

- You **MUST** be fit to drive (for example, you must be within the drink-drive legal limits and not be under the influence of drugs). See Rules 90 to 96.

- The vehicle **MUST** be road legal (for example, it must have an MOT certificate, if applicable, and it must be taxed and insured). The vehicle must be roadworthy (see Rules 89 and 97; and Annexes 3 and 6). You will also still be responsible for your passengers and anything else you are carrying (see Rules 98 to 102).

- You **MUST NOT** do anything illegal – like using a hand-held mobile phone, or similar hand-held device. There are exceptions to this, which are set out in Rule 149.

If a self-driving vehicle needs to hand control back to the driver, it will give you enough warning to do this safely. You **MUST** always be able and ready to take control, and do it when the vehicle prompts you. For example, you should stay in the driving seat and stay awake. When you have taken back control or turned off the self-driving function, you are responsible for all aspects of driving.

Laws RTA sections 2, 3, 4, 5, 5A, 14, 15 & AEVA section 1 & CUR regs 100, 104, 109 (as modified by the Road Vehicles (Construction and Use) (Automated Vehicles) Order 2022), 110

Hierarchy of road users

The 'hierarchy of road users' is a concept that places those road users most at risk in the event of a collision at the top of the hierarchy. The hierarchy does not remove the need for everyone to behave responsibly. The road users most likely to be injured in the event of a collision are pedestrians, cyclists, horse riders and motorcyclists, with children, older adults and disabled people being more at risk. The following H rules clarify this concept.

Rule H1

It is important that **ALL** road users are aware of *The Highway Code*, are considerate to other road users and understand their responsibility for the safety of others.

Everyone suffers when road collisions occur, whether they are physically injured or not. But those in charge of vehicles that can cause the greatest harm in the event of a collision bear the greatest responsibility to take care and reduce the danger they pose to others. This principle applies most strongly to drivers of large goods and passenger vehicles, vans/minibuses, cars/taxis and motorcycles.

Cyclists, horse riders and drivers of horse-drawn vehicles likewise have a responsibility to reduce danger to pedestrians.

None of this detracts from the responsibility of **ALL** road users, including pedestrians, cyclists and horse riders, to have regard for their own and other road users' safety.

Always remember that the people you encounter may have impaired sight, hearing or mobility and that this may not be obvious.

Rule H2
Rule for drivers, motorcyclists, horse-drawn vehicles, horse riders and cyclists

At a junction, you should give way to pedestrians crossing or waiting to cross a road into which or from which you are turning.

You **MUST** give way to pedestrians on a zebra crossing, and to pedestrians and cyclists on a parallel crossing (see Rule 195).

Pedestrians have priority when on a zebra crossing, on a parallel crossing or at light-controlled crossings when they have a green signal.

You should give way to pedestrians waiting to cross a zebra crossing, and to pedestrians and cyclists waiting to cross a parallel crossing.

Horse riders should also give way to pedestrians on a zebra crossing, and to pedestrians and cyclists on a parallel crossing.

Cyclists should give way to pedestrians on shared-use cycle tracks and to horse riders on bridleways.

Only pedestrians may use the pavement. Pedestrians include wheelchair and mobility scooter users.

Pedestrians may use any part of the road and use cycle tracks as well as the pavement, unless there are signs prohibiting pedestrians.

Laws TSRGD schedule 14 part 1 and part 5 & HA 1835 sect 72, R(S)A 1984, sect 129 & Countryside Act 1968 Sect 1 part 30

Rule H2
Wait for the pedestrian to cross the junction before turning. This applies if you are turning right or left into the junction

Rule H3
Rule for drivers and motorcyclists

You should not cut across cyclists, horse riders or horse-drawn vehicles going ahead when you are turning into or out of a junction or changing direction or lane, just as you would not turn across the path of another motor vehicle. This applies whether they are using a cycle lane, a cycle track, or riding ahead on the road and you should give way to them.

Do not turn at a junction if to do so would cause the cyclist, horse rider or horse-drawn vehicle going straight ahead to stop or swerve.

You should stop and wait for a safe gap in the flow of cyclists if necessary. This includes when cyclists are

- approaching, passing or moving off from a junction

- moving past or waiting alongside stationary or slow-moving traffic

- travelling around a roundabout.

Rule H3
Wait for the cyclist to pass the junction before turning. This also applies if there is a cycle lane or cycle track and if you are turning right or left into the junction

Rules for pedestrians

General guidance

1 **Pavements and footways** (including any path along the side of a road) should be used if provided. Where possible, avoid being next to the kerb with your back to the traffic. If you have to step into the road, look both ways first. Always remain aware of your environment and avoid unnecessary distractions. Always show due care and consideration for others.

2 **If there is no pavement,** keep to the right-hand side of the road so that you can see oncoming traffic. You should take extra care and

- be prepared to walk in single file, especially on narrow roads or in poor light
- keep close to the side of the road.

It may be safer to cross the road well before a sharp right-hand bend so that oncoming traffic has a better chance of seeing you. Cross back after the bend.

3 **Help other road users to see you.** Wear or carry something light-coloured, bright or fluorescent in poor daylight conditions. When it is dark, use reflective materials (e.g. armbands, sashes, waistcoats, jackets, footwear), which can be seen by drivers using headlights up to three times as far away as non-reflective materials.

Rule 3
Help yourself to be seen

4 **Young children** should not be out alone on the pavement or road (see Rule 7). When taking children out, keep between them and the traffic and hold their hands firmly. Strap very young children into pushchairs or use reins. When pushing a young child in a buggy, do not push the buggy into the road when checking to see if it is clear to cross, particularly from between parked vehicles.

5 **Organised walks or parades** involving large groups of people walking along a road should use a pavement if available; if one is not available, they should keep to the left. Look-outs should be positioned at the front and back of the group, and they should wear fluorescent clothes in daylight and reflective clothes in the dark. At night, the look-out in front should show a white light and the one at the back a red light. People on the outside of large groups should also carry lights and wear reflective clothing.

6 **Motorways.** Pedestrians **MUST NOT** be on motorways or slip roads except in an emergency (see Rules 272 and 277).
Laws RTRA sect 17, MT(E&W)R reg 15(1)(b) & MT(S)R reg 13

Crossing the road

7 **The Green Cross Code.** The advice given below on crossing the road is for all pedestrians. Children should be taught the Code and should not be allowed out alone until they can understand and use it properly. The age when they can do this is different for each child. Many children cannot judge how fast vehicles are going or how far away they are. Children learn by example, so parents and carers should always use the Code in full when out with their children. They are responsible for deciding at what age children can use it safely by themselves.

A First find a safe place to cross and where there is space to reach the pavement on the other side. Where there is a crossing nearby, use it. It is safer to cross using a subway, a footbridge, an island, a zebra, pelican, toucan or puffin crossing, or where there is a crossing point controlled by a police officer, a school crossing patrol or a traffic warden.

Otherwise choose a place where you can see clearly in all directions. Try to avoid crossing between parked cars (see Rule 14), on a blind bend, or close to the brow of a hill. Move to a space where drivers and riders can see you clearly. Do not cross the road diagonally.

Rule 7
Look all around and listen for traffic before crossing

B Stop just before you get to the kerb, where you can see if anything is coming. Do not get too close to the traffic. If there's no pavement, keep back from the edge of the road but make sure you can still see approaching traffic.

C Look all around for traffic and listen. Traffic could come from any direction. Listen as well, because you can sometimes hear traffic before you see it.

D If traffic is coming, let it pass. Look all around again and listen. Do not cross until there is a safe gap in the traffic and you are certain that there is plenty of time. Remember, even if traffic is a long way off, it may be approaching very quickly.

**E When it is safe, go straight across the road –
do not run.** Keep looking and listening for traffic while you cross, in case there is any traffic you did not see, or in case other traffic appears suddenly. Look out for cyclists and motorcyclists travelling between lanes of traffic. Do not walk diagonally across the road.

8 **At a junction.** When you are crossing or waiting to cross the road, other traffic should give way. Look out for traffic turning into the road, especially from behind you, and cross at a place where drivers can see you. If you have started crossing and traffic wants to turn into the road, you have priority and they should give way (see Rules H2 and 170).

9 **Pedestrian safety barriers.** Where there are barriers, cross the road only at the gaps provided for pedestrians. Do not climb over the barriers or walk between them and the road.

10 **Tactile paving.** Raised surfaces that can be felt underfoot provide warning and guidance to blind or partially sighted people. The most common surfaces are a series of raised studs, which are used at crossing points with a dropped kerb, or a series of rounded raised bars which are used at level crossings, at the top and bottom of steps and at some other hazards.

11 **One-way streets.** Check which way the traffic is moving. Do not cross until it is safe to do so without stopping. Bus and cycle lanes may operate in the opposite direction to the rest of the traffic.

12 **Bus and cycle lanes.** Take care when crossing these lanes as traffic may be moving faster than in the other lanes, or against the flow of traffic.

13 **Routes shared with cyclists.** Cycle tracks may run alongside footpaths or pavements and be separated from them by a feature such as a change of material, a verge, a kerb or a white line. Such routes may also incorporate short lengths of tactile paving to help visually impaired people stay on the correct side. On the pedestrian side, this may comprise a series of flat-topped bars running across the direction of travel (ladder pattern). On the cyclist side, the same bars are orientated in the direction of travel (tramline pattern).

Some routes shared with cyclists will not be separated by such a feature allowing cyclists and pedestrians to share the same space. Cyclists should respect your safety (see Rule 62), but you should also take care not to obstruct or endanger them. Always remain aware of your environment and avoid unnecessary distractions.

Where signs indicate, some routes are shared between pedestrians, cyclists, horse riders and horse-drawn vehicles. Cyclists, horse riders and drivers of horse-drawn vehicles should respect your safety, but you should take care not to obstruct or endanger them. Always remain aware of your environment and avoid unnecessary distractions.

14 **Parked vehicles.** If you have to cross between parked vehicles, use the outside edges of the vehicles as if they were the kerb. Stop there and make sure you can see all around and that the traffic can see you. Make sure there is a gap between any parked vehicles on the other side, so you can reach the pavement. Never cross the road in front of, or behind, any vehicle with its engine running, especially a large vehicle, as the driver may not be able to see you.

15 **Reversing vehicles.** Never cross behind a vehicle which is reversing, showing white reversing lights or sounding a warning.

16 **Moving vehicles.** You **MUST NOT** get onto or hold onto a moving vehicle.
Law RTA 1988 sect 26

17 **At night.** Wear something reflective to make it easier for others to see you (see Rule 3). If there is no pedestrian crossing nearby, cross the road near a street light so that traffic can see you more easily.

Crossings

18 **At all crossings.** When using any type of crossing you should

- always check that the traffic has stopped before you start to cross or push a pram onto a crossing
- always cross between the studs or over the zebra

markings. Do not cross at the side of the crossing or on the zig-zag lines, as it can be dangerous.

You **MUST NOT** loiter on any type of crossing.

Laws TSRGD schedule 14 part 5 & RTRA sect 25(5)

19 **Zebra crossings.** Give traffic plenty of time to see you and to stop before you start to cross. Vehicles will need more time when the road is slippery. Wait until traffic has stopped from both directions or the road is clear before crossing. Remember that traffic does not have to stop until someone has moved onto the crossing. Drivers and riders should give way to pedestrians waiting to cross and **MUST** give way to pedestrians on a zebra crossing (see Rule H2). Keep looking both ways, and listening, in case a driver or rider has not seen you and attempts to overtake a vehicle that has stopped.

Rule 19
Zebra crossings have flashing beacons

A zebra crossing with a central island is two separate crossings (see Rule 20).

Law TSRGD schedule 14 part 5

Rule 20
Zebra crossings with a central island are two separate crossings

20 Where there is an island in the middle of a zebra crossing, wait on the island and follow Rule 19 before you cross the second half of the road – it is a separate crossing.

21 **At traffic lights.** There may be special signals for pedestrians. You should only start to cross the road when the green figure shows. If you have started to cross the road and the green figure goes out, you should still have time to reach the other side, but do not delay. If no pedestrian signals have been provided, watch carefully and do not cross until the traffic lights are red and the traffic has stopped. Keep looking and check for traffic that may be turning the corner. Remember that traffic lights may let traffic move in some lanes while traffic in other lanes has stopped.

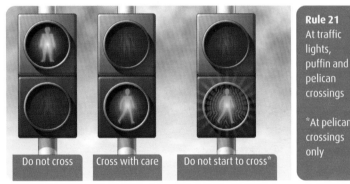

Do not cross   Cross with care   Do not start to cross*

Rule 21
At traffic lights, puffin and pelican crossings

*At pelican crossings only

22 **Pelican crossings.** These are signal-controlled crossings operated by pedestrians. Push the control button to activate the traffic signals. When the red figure shows, do not cross. When a steady green figure shows, check the traffic has stopped then cross with care. When the green figure begins to flash you should not start to cross. If you have already started you should have time to finish crossing safely.

23 **Puffin crossings** differ from pelican crossings as the red and green figures are above the control box on your side of the road and there is no flashing green figure phase. Press the button and wait for the green figure to show.

24 When the road is congested, traffic on your side of the road may be forced to stop even though their lights are green. Traffic may still be moving on the other side of the road, so press the button and wait for the signal to cross.

25 **Toucan crossings** are light-controlled crossings which allow cyclists and pedestrians to share crossing space and cross at the same time. They are push-button operated. Pedestrians and cyclists will see the green signal together. Cyclists are permitted to ride across.

Rule 25
Toucan crossings can be used by both cyclists and pedestrians

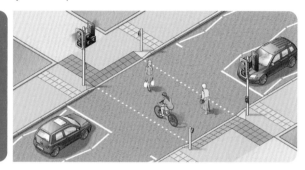

26 At some crossings there is a bleeping sound or voice signal to indicate to blind or partially sighted people when the steady green figure is showing, and there may be a tactile signal to help deafblind people.

27 **Equestrian crossings** are for horse riders. They have pavement barriers, wider crossing spaces, horse and rider figures in the light panels and either two sets of controls (one higher), or just one higher control panel.

Rule 27
Equestrian crossings are used by horse riders. There is often a parallel crossing

28 **'Staggered' pelican or puffin crossings.** When the crossings on each side of the central refuge are not in line they are two separate crossings. On reaching the central island, press the button again and wait for a steady green figure.

Rule 28
Staggered crossings (with an island in the middle) are two separate crossings

29 **Crossings controlled by an authorised person.** Do not cross the road unless you are signalled to do so by a police officer, traffic warden or school crossing patrol. Always cross in front of them.

30 Where there are no controlled crossing points available it is advisable to cross where there is an island in the middle of the road. Use the Green Cross Code (see Rule 7) to cross to the island and then stop and use it again to cross the second half of the road.

Situations needing extra care

31 **Emergency vehicles.** If an ambulance, fire engine, police or other emergency vehicle approaches using flashing blue lights, headlights and/or sirens, keep off the road.

32 **Buses.** Get on or off a bus only when it has stopped to allow you to do so. Watch out for cyclists when you are getting off. Never cross the road directly behind or in front of a bus. Wait until it has moved off and you can see clearly in both directions.

33 **Tramways.** These may run through pedestrian areas. Their path will be marked out by shallow kerbs, changes in the paving or other road surface, white lines or yellow dots. Cross at designated crossings where provided. Elsewhere treat trams as you would other road vehicles and look both ways along the track before crossing. Do not walk along the track as trams may come up behind you. Trams move quietly and cannot steer to avoid you.

34 **Railway level crossings.** You **MUST NOT** cross or pass a stop line when the red lights show, (including a red pedestrian figure). Also do not cross if an alarm is sounding or the barriers are being lowered. The tone of the alarm may change if another train is approaching. If there are no lights, alarms or barriers, stop, look both ways and listen before crossing. A tactile surface comprising rounded bars running across the direction of pedestrian travel may be installed on the footpath approaching a level crossing to warn visually impaired people of its presence. The tactile surface should extend across the full width of the footway and should be located at an appropriate distance from the barrier or projected line of the barrier.

Law TSRGD schedule 14 part 1

35 **Street and pavement repairs.** A pavement may be closed temporarily because it is not safe to use. Take extra care if you are directed to walk in or to cross the road.

Where should horse riders be when using roundabouts?

Turn to Rule 186 (pages 74–75)

Rules for users of powered wheelchairs and powered mobility scooters

(Called Invalid Carriages in law)

36 There is one class of manual wheelchair (called a Class 1 invalid carriage) and two classes of powered wheelchairs and powered mobility scooters. Manual wheelchairs and Class 2 vehicles are those with an upper speed limit of 4 mph (6 km/h) and are designed to be used on pavements. Class 3 vehicles are those with an upper speed limit of 8 mph (12 km/h) and are equipped to be used on the road as well as the pavement.

37 When you are on the road you should obey the guidance and rules for other vehicles; when on the pavement you should follow the guidance and rules for pedestrians.

On pavements

38 Pavements are safer than roads and should be used when available. You should give pedestrians priority and show consideration for other pavement users, particularly those with a hearing or visual impairment who may not be aware that you are there.

39 Powered wheelchairs and scooters **MUST NOT** travel faster than 4 mph (6 km/h) on pavements or in pedestrian areas. You may need to reduce your speed to adjust to other pavement users who may not be able to move out of your way quickly enough or where the pavement is too narrow.
Law UICHR reg 4

40 When moving off the pavement onto the road, you should take special care. Before moving off, always look round and make sure it's safe to join the traffic. Always try to use dropped kerbs when moving off the pavement, even if this means travelling further to locate one. If you have to climb or descend a kerb, always approach it at right angles and don't try to negotiate a kerb higher than the vehicle manufacturer's recommendations.

On the road

41 You should take care when travelling on the road as you may be travelling more slowly than other traffic (your machine is restricted to 8 mph (12 km/h) and may be less visible).

42 When on the road, Class 3 vehicles should travel in the direction of the traffic. Class 2 users should always use the pavement when it is available. When there is no pavement, you should use caution when on the road. Class 2 users should, where possible, travel in the direction of the traffic. If you are travelling at night when lights **MUST** be used, you should travel in the direction of the traffic to avoid confusing other road users.

Law UICHR reg 9

43 You **MUST** follow the same rules about using lights, indicators and horns as for other road vehicles, if your vehicle is fitted with them. At night, lights **MUST** be used. Be aware that other road users may not see you and you should make yourself more visible – even in the daytime and also at dusk – by, for instance, wearing a reflective jacket or reflective strips on the back of the vehicle.

Law UICHR reg 9

What should you do if the traffic lights are not working?

Turn to Rule 176 (pages 70–71)

44 Take extra care at road junctions. When going straight ahead, check to make sure there are no vehicles about to cross your path from the left, the right, or overtaking you and turning left. There are several options for dealing with right turns, especially turning from a major road. If moving into the middle of the road is difficult or dangerous, you can

- stop on the left-hand side of the road and wait for a safe gap in the traffic
- negotiate the turn as a pedestrian, i.e. travel along the pavement and cross the road between pavements where it is safe to do so. Class 3 users should switch the vehicle to the lower speed limit when on pavements.

If the junction is too hazardous, it may be worth considering an alternative route. Similarly, when negotiating major roundabouts (i.e. with two or more lanes) it may be safer for you to use the pavement or find a route which avoids the roundabout altogether.

45 All normal parking restrictions should be observed. Your vehicle should not be left unattended if it causes an obstruction to other pedestrians – especially those in wheelchairs. Parking concessions provided under the Blue Badge scheme (see Further reading) will apply to those vehicles displaying a valid badge.

46 These vehicles **MUST NOT** be used on motorways (see Rule 253). They should not be used on unrestricted dual carriageways where the speed limit exceeds 50 mph (80 km/h) but if they are used on these dual carriageways, they **MUST** have a flashing amber beacon. A flashing amber beacon should be used on all other dual carriageways (see Rule 220).

Laws RTRA sects 17(2) & (3) & RVLR regs 17(1) & 26

Rules about animals

Horse-drawn vehicles

47 Horse-drawn vehicles used on the highway should be operated and maintained in accordance with standards set out in the Department for Transport's Code of Practice for Horse-Drawn Vehicles. This Code lays down the requirements for a road driving assessment and includes a comprehensive list of safety checks to ensure that a carriage and its fittings are safe and in good working order. The standards set out in the Road Driving Assessment may be required to be met by a Local Authority if an operator wishes to obtain a local authority licence to operate a passenger-carrying service (see Further reading).

48 **Safety equipment and clothing.** All horse-drawn vehicles should have two red rear reflectors. It is safer not to drive at night but if you do, a light showing white to the front and red to the rear **MUST** be fitted.

Law RVLR reg 4

Horse riders

49 **Safety equipment.** Children under the age of 14 **MUST** wear a helmet which complies with the Regulations. It **MUST** be fastened securely. Other riders should also follow these requirements. These requirements do not apply to a child who is a follower of the Sikh religion while wearing a turban.

Laws H(PHYR)A sect 1 & H(PHYR)R reg 3

50 **Other clothing.** You should wear

- boots or shoes with hard soles and heels
- light-coloured or fluorescent clothing in daylight
- reflective clothing if you have to ride at night or in poor visibility.

Rule 50
Help yourself to be seen

51 **At night.** It is safer not to ride on the road at night or in poor visibility, but if you do, make sure you wear reflective clothing and your horse has reflective bands above the fetlock joints. A light which shows white to the front and red to the rear should be fitted, with a band, to the rider's right arm and/or leg/riding boot. If you are leading a horse at night, carry a light in your right hand, showing white to the front and red to the rear, and wear reflective clothing on both you and your horse. It is strongly recommended that a fluorescent/reflective tail guard is also worn by your horse.

Riding

52 Before you take a horse or horse-drawn vehicle on to the road, you should

- ensure all tack fits well and is in good condition

- make sure you can control your horse.

If you are an inexperienced horse rider or have not ridden for a while, consider taking the Ride Safe Award from The British Horse Society. The Ride Safe Award provides a foundation for any horse rider to be safe and knowledgeable when riding in all environments, but particularly on the road. For more information, see www.bhs.org.uk

Always ride with other, less nervous horses if you think that your horse will be nervous of traffic. Never ride a horse without both a saddle and bridle.

53 Before riding off or turning, look behind you to make sure it is safe, then give a clear arm signal.

When riding on the road, you should

- keep to the left
- keep both hands on the reins unless you are signalling
- keep both feet in the stirrups
- not carry another person
- not carry anything which might affect your balance or get tangled up with the reins
- keep a horse you are leading to your left
- move in the direction of the traffic flow in a one-way street
- never ride more than two abreast, and ride in single file on narrow or busy roads and when riding round bends.

54 You **MUST NOT** take a horse onto a footpath or pavement, and you should not take a horse onto a cycle track. Use a bridleway where possible. Equestrian crossings may be provided for horse riders to cross the road and you should use these where available (see Rule 27). You should dismount at level crossings where a 'Horse Rider Dismount' sign is displayed.

Laws HA 1835 sect 72 & R(S)A sect 129(5)

55 Avoid roundabouts wherever possible. If you use them, you should

- keep to the left and watch out for vehicles crossing your path to leave or join the roundabout
- signal right when riding across exits to show you are not leaving
- signal left just before you leave the roundabout.

Other animals

56 **Dogs.** Do not let a dog out on the road on its own. Keep it on a short lead when walking on the pavement, road or path shared with cyclists or horse riders.

57 When in a vehicle make sure dogs or other animals are suitably restrained so they cannot distract you while you are driving or injure you, or themselves, if you stop quickly. A seat belt harness, pet carrier, dog cage or dog guard are ways of restraining animals in cars.

58 **Animals being herded.** These should be kept under control at all times. You should, if possible, send another person along the road in front to warn other road users, especially at a bend or the brow of a hill. It is safer not to move animals after dark, but if you do, then wear reflective clothing and ensure that lights are carried (white at the front and red at the rear of the herd).

Rules for cyclists

These rules are in addition to those in the following sections, which apply to all vehicles (except the motorway section, Rules 253–274). See also Annex 1.

59 **Clothing.** You should avoid clothes that may get tangled in the chain, or in a wheel or may obscure your lights when you are cycling.

Light-coloured or fluorescent clothing can help other road users to see you in daylight and poor light, while reflective clothing and/or accessories (belt, arm or ankle bands) can increase your visibility in the dark.

You should wear a cycle helmet that conforms to current regulations, is the correct size and securely fastened. Evidence suggests that a correctly fitted helmet will reduce your risk of sustaining a head injury in certain circumstances.

60 **At night** your cycle **MUST** have white front and red rear lights lit. It **MUST** also be fitted with a red rear reflector (and amber pedal reflectors, if manufactured after 1/10/85). White front reflectors and spoke reflectors will also help you to be seen. Flashing lights are permitted but it is recommended that cyclists who are riding in areas without street lighting use a steady front lamp.

Law RVLR regs 13, 18 & 24

61 **Cycle routes and other facilities.** Cycle lanes are marked by a white line (which may be broken) along the carriageway (see Rule 140). Use facilities such as cycle lanes and tracks, advanced stop lines and toucan crossings (see Rules 62 and 73) where they make your journey safer and easier. This will depend on your experience and skills and the situation at the time. While such facilities are provided for reasons of safety, cyclists may exercise their judgement and are not obliged to use them.

62 **Cycle tracks.** These are routes for cyclists that are physically protected or located away from motor traffic, other than where they cross side roads (see Rule 206). Cycle tracks may run alongside footpaths or pavements and be separated by a feature such as a change of material, a verge, a kerb or a white line. You **MUST** keep to the side intended for cyclists as the pedestrian side remains a pavement or footpath.

Some cycle tracks shared with pedestrians will not be separated by such a feature. On such shared-use routes, you should always take care when passing pedestrians, especially children, older adults or disabled people, and allow them plenty of room. Always be prepared to slow down and stop if necessary (see Rule H2).

Law HA 1835 sect 72

63 **Sharing space with pedestrians, horse riders and horse-drawn vehicles.** When riding in places where sharing with pedestrians, horse riders or horse-drawn vehicles is permitted, take care when passing pedestrians and horse riders, especially children, older adults or disabled people. Slow down when necessary and let them know you are there; for example, by ringing your bell (it is recommended that a bell is fitted to your bike) or by calling out politely.

Remember that pedestrians may be deaf, blind or partially sighted and that this may not be obvious.

Do not pass pedestrians, horse riders or horse-drawn vehicles closely or at high speed, particularly from behind. You should not pass a horse on their left. Remember that horses can be startled if passed without warning. Always be prepared to slow down and stop when necessary.

64 You **MUST NOT** cycle on a pavement.

Laws HA 1835 sect 72 & R(S)A sect 129

65 **Bus lanes.** Most bus lanes may be used by cyclists as indicated on signs. Watch out for people getting on or off a bus. Be very careful when overtaking a bus or leaving a bus lane as you will be entering a busier traffic flow. Do not pass between the kerb and a bus when it is at a stop.

66 You should

- avoid any actions that could reduce your control of your cycle

- be considerate of the needs of other road users when riding in groups. You can ride two abreast and it can be safer to do so, particularly in larger groups or when accompanying children or less experienced riders. Be aware of drivers behind you and allow them to overtake (for example, by moving into single file or stopping) when you feel it is safe to let them do so

- not ride close behind another vehicle in case it stops suddenly

- not carry anything that will affect your balance or may get tangled up with your wheels or chain

- be considerate of other road users, particularly blind and partially sighted pedestrians, and horse riders (see Rule H1). Let them know you are there when necessary; for example, by calling out or ringing your bell if you have one. It is recommended that a bell be fitted.

67

You should

- look all around to make sure it is safe before moving away from the kerb, when pulling out to overtake or to pass stationary vehicles, or when turning at junctions or stopping

- watch out for obstructions in the road, such as drains, service covers and potholes, positioning yourself so you can move to the left (as well as to the right) to avoid them safely

- take care when passing parked vehicles, leaving enough room (a door's width or 1 metre) to avoid being hit if a car door is opened, and watch out for pedestrians stepping into your path

- be aware of traffic coming up behind you, including other cyclists, and give a clear signal to show other road users what you intend to do (see Signals to other road users)

- take extra care near road humps, narrowings and other traffic-calming features

- when cycling on the road, only pass to the left of large vehicles when they are stationary or slow moving and you should proceed with caution as the driver may not be able to see you. Be particularly careful on the approach to junctions or where a large vehicle could change lanes to the left.

You **MUST NOT**

- carry a passenger unless your cycle has been built or adapted to carry one
- hold onto a moving vehicle or trailer
- ride in a dangerous, careless or inconsiderate manner
- ride when under the influence of drink or drugs, including medicine.

Law RTA 1988 sects 24, 26, 28, 29 & 30 as amended by RTA 1991

You **MUST** obey all traffic signs and traffic light signals.

Laws RTA 1988 sect 36 & TSRGD schedule 3 part 3, schedule 7 part 4, schedule 9 parts 4 and 6, schedule 13 part 6, schedule 14 part 2

When parking your cycle

- find a conspicuous location where it can be seen by passers-by
- use cycle stands or other cycle parking facilities wherever possible
- do not leave it where it would cause an obstruction or hazard to other road users
- secure it well so that it will not fall over and become an obstruction or hazard.

At traffic light junctions and at cycle-only crossings with traffic lights, you **MUST NOT** cross the stop line when the lights are red.

Some junctions have an advanced stop line to enable you to position yourself ahead of other traffic and wait (see Rule 178). When the traffic lights are red, you may cross the first stop line, but you **MUST NOT** cross the final stop line.

Laws RTA 1988 sect 36 & TSRGD schedule 14 part 1

72 **Road positioning.** When riding on the roads, there are two basic road positions you should adopt, depending on the situation.

1. Ride in the centre of your lane, to make yourself as clearly visible as possible, in the following situations

   • on quiet roads or streets – if a faster vehicle comes up behind you, move to the left to enable them to overtake, if you can do so safely

   • in slower-moving traffic – when the traffic around you starts to flow more freely, move over to the left if you can do so safely so that faster vehicles behind you can overtake

   • at the approach to junctions or road narrowings where it would be unsafe for drivers to overtake you.

2. When riding on busy roads with vehicles moving faster than you, allow them to overtake where it is safe to do so whilst keeping at least 0.5 metres away, and further where it is safer, from the kerb edge. Remember that traffic on most dual carriageways moves quickly. Take extra care crossing slip roads.

Road junctions

73 **Junctions.** Some junctions, particularly those with traffic lights, have special cycle facilities, including small cycle traffic lights at eye-level height, which may allow you to move or cross separately from or ahead of other traffic. Use these facilities where they make your journey safer and easier.

At junctions with no separate cyclist facilities, it is recommended that you proceed as if you were driving a motor vehicle (see Rules 170 to 190). Position yourself in the centre of your chosen lane, where you feel able to do this safely, to make yourself as visible as possible and to avoid being overtaken where this would be dangerous. If you do not feel safe to proceed in this way, you may prefer to dismount and wheel your bike across the junction.

74 **Turning.** When approaching a junction on the left, watch out for vehicles turning in front of you, out of or into the side road. If you intend to turn left, check first for other cyclists or motorcyclists before signalling. Do not ride on the inside of vehicles signalling or slowing down to turn left.

If you are turning right, check the traffic to ensure it is safe, then signal and move to the centre of the road. Wait until there is a safe gap in the oncoming traffic and give a final look before completing the turn. It may be safer to wait on the left until there is a safe gap or to dismount and push your cycle across the road.

When turning into or out of a side road, you should give way to pedestrians crossing or waiting to cross (see Rule H2).

75 **Two-stage turns.** At some signal-controlled junctions, there may be signs and markings informing cyclists to turn right in two stages

Stage 1: When the traffic lights turn green, cyclists wishing to make the turn should go straight ahead to the location marked by a cycle symbol and turn arrow on the carriageway; then stop and wait there.

Stage 2: When the traffic lights on the far side of the junction, now facing the cyclists, turn green, they should then complete the manoeuvre.

76 **Going straight ahead.** If you are going straight ahead at a junction, you have priority over traffic waiting to turn into or out of the side road, unless road signs or markings indicate otherwise (see Rule H3). Check that you can proceed safely, particularly when approaching junctions on the left alongside stationary or slow-moving traffic. Watch out for drivers intending to turn across your path. Remember the driver ahead may not be able to see you, so bear in mind your speed and position in the road.

Take great care when deciding whether it is safe to pass stationary or slow-moving lorries and other long vehicles, especially at the approach to junctions, as their drivers may not be able to see you. Remember that they may have to move over to the right before turning left, and that their rear wheels may then come very close to the kerb while turning (see Rule 67).

77 **Busy roads.** When crossing faster or busy main roads, you may find it safer and easier to

- dismount and push your cycle across
- wait for a safe gap in the traffic before doing so, especially on faster roads and dual carriageways
- make use of traffic islands or central reservations to help you where appropriate.

Roundabouts

78 Full details about the correct procedure at roundabouts without cycle facilities are contained in Rules 184 to 190.

Watch out for vehicles crossing your path to leave or join the roundabout, remembering that drivers may not easily see you.

79 If you are turning right, you can ride in the left or right-hand lanes and move left when approaching your exit. Position yourself in the centre of your lane if it is safe to do so (see Rule 72) and signal right to indicate that you are not leaving the roundabout. Alternatively, you may feel safer walking your cycle round on the pavement or verge.

If you decide to ride round keeping to the left-hand lane, you should

- be aware that drivers may not easily see you
- take extra care when cycling across exits. You should signal right to show you are not leaving the roundabout
- watch out for vehicles crossing your path to leave or join the roundabout.

Where a roundabout has separate cycle facilities, you should use these facilities where they make your journey safer and easier although you are not obliged to use them. This will depend on your experience and skills and the situation at the time.

80 Give plenty of room to long vehicles on the roundabout as they need more space to manoeuvre. Do not ride in the space they need to get round the roundabout. It may be safer to wait until they have cleared the roundabout.

Crossing the road

81 Do not ride across equestrian crossings, as they are for horse riders only. Do not ride across a pelican, puffin or zebra crossing. Dismount and wheel your cycle across.

82 **Crossings.** Toucan crossings are light-controlled crossings that allow cyclists and pedestrians to share crossing space and cross at the same time. They are push-button operated. Pedestrians and cyclists will see the green signal together. Cyclists are permitted to ride across.

Cycle tracks on opposite sides of the road may be linked by cycle-only signalled crossings. You may ride across but you **MUST NOT** cross until the green cycle symbol is showing.

Cycle track crossings can be in spacious pedestrian environments. Cyclists should look out and be prepared to stop for pedestrians crossing the track informally as well as at these designated points.

Take extra care when crossing level crossings and tramways (see Rule 306). You should dismount at level crossings where a 'Cyclist Dismount' sign is displayed.

Law TSRGD schedule 14 part 1

Rules for motorcyclists

These Rules are in addition to those in the following sections which apply to all vehicles. For motorcycle licence requirements, see Annex 2.

83 On all journeys, the rider and pillion passenger on a motorcycle, scooter or moped **MUST** wear a protective helmet. This does not apply to a follower of the Sikh religion while wearing a turban. Helmets **MUST** comply with the Regulations and they **MUST** be fastened securely. Riders and passengers of motor tricycles and quadricycles, also called quadbikes, should also wear a protective helmet. Before each journey check that your helmet visor is clean and in good condition.

Laws RTA 1988 sects 16 & 17, & MC(PH)R as amended reg 4

84 It is also advisable to wear eye protectors, which **MUST** comply with the Regulations. Scratched or poorly fitting eye protectors can limit your view when riding, particularly in bright sunshine and the hours of darkness. Consider wearing ear protection. Strong boots, gloves and suitable clothing may help to protect you if you are involved in a collision.

Laws RTA 1988 sect 18 & MC(EP)R as amended reg 4

85 You **MUST NOT** carry more than one pillion passenger who **MUST** sit astride the machine on a proper seat. They should face forward with both feet on the footrests. You **MUST NOT** carry a pillion passenger unless your motor cycle is designed to do so. Provisional licence holders **MUST NOT** carry a pillion passenger.

Laws RTA 1988 sect 23, MV(DL)R reg 16(6) & CUR reg 102

86 **Daylight riding.** Make yourself as visible as possible from the side as well as the front and rear. You could wear a light or brightly coloured helmet and fluorescent clothing or strips. Dipped headlights, even in good daylight, may also make you more conspicuous. However, be aware that other vehicle drivers may still not have seen you, or judged your distance or speed correctly, especially at junctions.

Rule 86
Help yourself to be seen

87 **Riding in the dark.** Wear reflective clothing or strips to improve your visibility in the dark. These reflect light from the headlamps of other vehicles, making you visible from a longer distance. See Rules 113–116 for lighting requirements.

88 **Manoeuvring.** You should be aware of what is behind and to the sides before manoeuvring. Look behind you; use mirrors if they are fitted. When in traffic queues look out for pedestrians crossing between vehicles and vehicles emerging from junctions or changing lanes. Position yourself so that drivers can see you in their mirrors. Additionally, when filtering in slow-moving traffic, take care and keep your speed low.
Remember: Observation – Signal – Manoeuvre

Rules for drivers and motorcyclists

89 **Vehicle condition.** You **MUST** ensure your vehicle and trailer comply with the full requirements of the Road Vehicles (Construction and Use) Regulations and Road Vehicles Lighting Regulations (see Annex 4).

Fitness to drive

90 Make sure that you are fit to drive. You **MUST** report to the Driver and Vehicle Licensing Agency (DVLA) any health condition likely to affect your driving.
Law RTA 1988 sect 94

91 Driving when you are tired greatly increases your risk of collision. To minimise this risk

- make sure you are fit to drive. Do not begin a journey if you are tired. Get sufficient sleep before embarking on a long journey
- avoid undertaking long journeys between midnight and 6 am, when natural alertness is at a minimum

- plan your journey to take sufficient breaks. A minimum break of at least 15 minutes after every two hours of driving is recommended
- if you feel sleepy, stop in a safe place. Do not stop in an emergency area or on a hard shoulder of a motorway (see Rule 262 for guidance on places to take a break when travelling on motorways).

92 **Vision.** You **MUST** be able to read a vehicle number plate, in good daylight, from a distance of 20 metres (or 20.5 metres where the old style number plate is used). If you need to wear glasses (or contact lenses) to do this, you **MUST** wear them at all times while driving. The police have the power to require a driver to undertake an eyesight test.

Laws RTA 1988 sect 96, & MV(DL)R reg 40 & sched 8

93 Slow down, and if necessary stop, if you are dazzled by bright sunlight.

94 At night or in poor visibility, do not use tinted glasses, lenses or visors if they restrict your vision.

Alcohol and drugs

95 **Do not drink and drive** as it will seriously affect your judgement and abilities. In England and Wales you **MUST NOT** drive with a breath alcohol level higher than 35 microgrammes/100 millilitres of breath or a blood alcohol level of more than 80 milligrammes/100 millilitres of blood. In Scotland the legal limits are lower. You **MUST NOT** drive with a breath alcohol level of more than 22 microgrammes/100 millilitres of breath or a blood alcohol level of more than 50 milligrammes/100 millilitres of blood.

Alcohol will

- give a false sense of confidence
- reduce co-ordination and slow down reactions
- affect judgement of speed, distance and risk
- reduce your driving ability, even if you're below the legal limit

- take time to leave your body; you may be unfit to drive in the evening after drinking at lunchtime, or in the morning after drinking the previous evening.

The best solution is not to drink at all when planning to drive because any amount of alcohol affects your ability to drive safely. If you are going to drink, arrange another means of transport.

Laws RTA 1988 sects 4, 5 & 11(2), & PLSR

96
You **MUST NOT** drive under the influence of drugs or medicine. For medicines, check with your doctor or pharmacist and do not drive if you are advised that you may be impaired.

You **MUST NOT** drive if you have illegal drugs or certain medicines in your blood above specified limits. It is highly dangerous so never take illegal drugs if you intend to drive; the effects are unpredictable, but can be even more severe than alcohol and result in fatal or serious road crashes. Illegal drugs have been specified at very low levels so even small amounts of use could be above the specified limits. The limits for certain medicines have been specified at higher levels, above the levels generally found in the blood of patients who have taken normal therapeutic doses. If you are found to have a concentration of a drug above its specified limit in your blood because you have been prescribed or legitimately supplied a particularly high dose of medicine, then you can raise a statutory medical defence, provided your driving was not impaired by the medicine you are taking.

Law RTA 1988 sects 4 & 5

Before setting off

Before setting off. You **MUST** ensure that

- you have a valid licence and insurance to drive the vehicle you intend to use (see Annex 3)
- your vehicle is legal and roadworthy (see Annexes 3 and 6 for important vehicle maintenance and safety checks).

You **SHOULD** ensure that

- you have planned your route and allowed sufficient time for breaks and possible delays

- you have sufficient fuel or charge for your journey, especially if it includes motorway driving

- you know where all the controls are and how to use them

- clothing and footwear do not prevent you using the controls in the correct manner

- your mirrors and seat are adjusted correctly to ensure comfort, full control and maximum vision

- head restraints are properly adjusted to reduce the risk of neck and spine injuries in the event of a collision.

It is recommended for emergency use that

- you have a mobile telephone containing emergency contacts (e.g. breakdown assistance)

- you have high-visibility clothing.

Laws RTA 1988 sects 42, 45, 47, 49, 53, 87, 99(4) & 143, MV(DL)R reg 16, 40 & sched 4, VERA sect 29, RVLR 1989 regs 23 & 27, & CUR regs 27, 30, 32 & 61

Rule 97
Make sure head restraints are properly adjusted

Vehicle towing and loading
98
Before towing. As a driver

- you **MUST NOT** tow more than your licence permits. If you passed your car driving test on or after 1 January 1997, you are restricted on the weight of trailer you can tow

- you **MUST** ensure that both your vehicle and your trailer are in a roadworthy condition. This includes checking that all tyres are legal, the trailer braking system is in full working order and all trailer lights are working correctly

- you **MUST NOT** overload your vehicle or trailer. You should not tow a weight greater than that recommended by the manufacturer of your vehicle

- you should distribute the weight in your caravan or trailer evenly with heavy items over the axle(s) and ensure a downward load on the tow ball. The manufacturer's recommended weight and tow ball load should not be exceeded. This should minimise the possibility of swerving or snaking and loss of control

- you **MUST** secure your load and it **MUST NOT** stick out dangerously. Make sure any heavy or sharp objects and any animals are secured safely. If there is a collision, they might hit someone inside the vehicle and cause serious injury

- if your vehicle is narrower than your trailer or load, or your trailer or load obstructs your rearward view, then towing mirrors **MUST** be used

- your trailer **MUST** be fitted with a secondary coupling device, such as a safety chain

- carrying a load or pulling a trailer may require you to adjust your headlights.

During towing. As a driver

- you should be aware that reduced speed limits apply (see Rule 124)

- you should be aware that your stopping distance may increase significantly when towing (see Rule 126)

- you **MUST NOT** drive in the right-hand lane on motorways with three or more lanes (see Rule 265)

- if the trailer starts to swerve or snake, or you lose control, ease off the accelerator and reduce speed gently to regain control. Do not brake harshly.

Breakdowns. In the event of a breakdown, be aware

- that towing a vehicle on a tow rope is potentially dangerous. You should consider using a solid tow bar or professional recovery

- it may take longer to build up speed when rejoining a carriageway (see also Rule 278).

For additional advice about towing safely, see Further reading.

Laws CUR regs 27, 33, 86a & 100, RVLR reg 18, MT(E&W)R reg 12 & MV(DL)R reg 6, 7, 76 & sched 2

Seat belts and child restraints

99 You **MUST** wear a seat belt in cars, vans and other goods vehicles if one is fitted (see table below). Adults, and children aged 14 years and over, **MUST** use a seat belt or child restraint, where fitted, when seated in minibuses, buses and coaches. Exemptions are allowed for the holders of medical exemption certificates and those making deliveries or collections in goods vehicles when travelling less than 50 metres (approx 162 feet).

Laws RTA 1988 sects 14 & 15, MV(WSB)R, MV(WSBCFS)R & MV(WSB)(A)R 2005 & 2006

Seat belt requirements. This table summarises the main legal requirements for wearing seat belts in cars, vans and other goods vehicles.

	Front seat	Rear seat	Who is responsible?
Driver	Seat belt **MUST** be worn if fitted	–	**Driver**
Child under 3 years of age	Correct child restraint **MUST** be used	Correct child restraint **MUST** be used. If one is not available in a taxi, may travel unrestrained	**Driver**
Child from 3rd birthday up to 1.35 metres in height (or 12th birthday, whichever they reach first)	Correct child restraint **MUST** be used	Correct child restraint **MUST** be used where seat belts fitted. **MUST** use adult belt if correct child restraint is not available in a licensed taxi or private hire vehicle, or for reasons of unexpected necessity over a short distance, or if two occupied restraints prevent fitment of a third	**Driver**
Child over 1.35 metres (approx 4ft 5 ins) in height or 12 or 13 years	Seat belt **MUST** be worn if available	Seat belt **MUST** be worn if available	**Driver**
Adult passengers aged 14 and over	Seat belt **MUST** be worn if available	Seat belt **MUST** be worn if available	**Passenger**

100 The driver **MUST** ensure that all children under 14 years of age in cars, vans and other goods vehicles wear seat belts or sit in an approved child restraint where required (see table above). If a child is under 1.35 metres (approx

4 feet 5 inches) tall, a baby seat, child seat, booster seat
or booster cushion **MUST** be used suitable for the child's
weight and fitted to the manufacturer's instructions.

Laws RTA 1988 sects 14 & 15, MV(WSB)R, MV(WSBCFS)R &
MV(WSB)(A)R 2006

Rule 100
Make sure
that a
child uses
a suitable
restraint
which is
correctly
adjusted

 A rear-facing baby seat **MUST NOT** be fitted into a seat
protected by an active frontal airbag, as in a crash it can
cause serious injury or death to the child.

Laws RTA 1988 sects 14 & 15, MV(WSB)R, MV(WSBCFS)R
& MV(WSB)(A)R 2006

102 **Children in cars, vans and other goods vehicles.**
Drivers who are carrying children in cars, vans and other
goods vehicles should also ensure that

- children should get into the vehicle through the door
  nearest the kerb

- child restraints are properly fitted to manufacturer's
  instructions

- children do not sit behind the rear seats in an estate car
  or hatchback, unless a special child seat has been fitted

- the child safety door locks, where fitted, are used when
  children are in the vehicle

- children are kept under control.

General rules, techniques and advice for all drivers and riders

This section should be read by all drivers, motorcyclists, cyclists and horse riders. The rules in *The Highway Code* do not give you the right of way in any circumstance, but they advise you when you should give way to others. Always give way if it can help to avoid an incident.

Signals

 Signals warn and inform other road users, including pedestrians (see Signals to other road users), of your intended actions. You should always

- give clear signals in plenty of time, having checked it is not misleading to signal at that time

- use them to advise other road users before changing course or direction, stopping or moving off

- cancel them after use

- make sure your signals will not confuse others. If, for instance, you want to stop after a side road, do not signal until you are passing the road. If you signal earlier it may give the impression that you intend to turn into the road. Your brake lights will warn traffic behind you that you are slowing down

- use an arm signal to emphasise or reinforce your signal if necessary. Remember that signalling does not give you priority.

 You should also

- watch out for signals given by other road users and proceed only when you are satisfied that it is safe

- be aware that an indicator on another vehicle may not have been cancelled.

You **MUST** obey signals given by police officers, traffic officers, traffic wardens (see Signals by authorised persons) and signs used by school crossing patrols.

Laws RTRA sect 28, RTA 1988 sect 35, TMA sect 6 & FTWO art 3

Police stopping procedures. If the police want to stop your vehicle they will, where possible, attract your attention by

- flashing blue lights, headlights or sounding their siren or horn, usually from behind

- directing you to pull over to the side by pointing and/or using the left indicator.

You **MUST** then pull over and stop as soon as it is safe to do so. Then switch off your engine.

Law RTA 1988 sect 163

Other stopping procedures

Driver and Vehicle Standards Agency officers have powers to stop vehicles on all roads, including motorways and trunk roads. They will attract your attention by flashing amber lights

- either from the front requesting you to follow them to a safe place to stop

- or from behind directing you to pull over to the side by pointing and/or using the left indicator.

It is an offence not to comply with their directions. You **MUST** obey any signals given (see Signals by authorised persons).

Laws RTA 1988 sect 67, & PRA sect 41 & sched 5(8)

Traffic officers have powers to stop vehicles on most motorways and some 'A' class roads in England and Wales. If traffic officers in uniform want to stop your vehicle on safety grounds (e.g. an insecure load) they will, where possible, attract your attention by

- flashing amber lights, usually from behind

- directing you to pull over to the side by pointing and/or using the left indicator.

You **MUST** then pull over and stop as soon as it is safe to do so. Then switch off your engine. It is an offence not to comply with their directions (see Signals by authorised persons).

Law RTA 1988 sects 35 & 163 as amended by TMA sect 6

109 **Traffic light signals and traffic signs.** You **MUST** obey all traffic light signals (see Light signals controlling traffic) and traffic signs giving orders, including temporary signals and signs (see Traffic signs). Make sure you know, understand and act on all other traffic and information signs and road markings (see Traffic signs, Road markings and Vehicle markings).

Laws RTA 1988 sect 36 & TSRGD schedule 3 part 4, schedule 9 parts 7 and 8, schedule 14 parts 1 and 5, schedule 7 part 6, schedule 15 part 1

110 **Flashing headlights.** Only flash your headlights to let other road users know that you are there. Do not flash your headlights to convey any other message or intimidate other road users.

111 Never assume that flashing headlights is a signal inviting you to proceed. Use your own judgement and proceed carefully.

112 **The horn.** Use only while your vehicle is moving and you need to warn other road users of your presence. Never sound your horn aggressively. You **MUST NOT** use your horn

- while stationary on the road

- when driving in a built-up area between the hours of 11.30 pm and 7.00 am

except when another road user poses a danger.

Law CUR reg 99

Lighting requirements

113 You **MUST**

- ensure all sidelights and rear registration plate lights are lit between sunset and sunrise

- use headlights at night, except on a road which has lit street lighting. These roads are generally restricted to a speed limit of 30 mph (48 km/h) unless otherwise specified

- use headlights when visibility is seriously reduced (see Rule 226).

Night (the hours of darkness) is defined as the period between half an hour after sunset and half an hour before sunrise.

Laws RVLR regs 3, 24 & 25 (In Scotland – RTRA sect 82 (as amended by NRSWA, para 59 of sched 8))

You **MUST NOT**

- use any lights in a way which would dazzle or cause discomfort to other road users, including pedestrians, cyclists and horse riders

- use front or rear fog lights unless visibility is seriously reduced. You **MUST** switch them off when visibility improves to avoid dazzling other road users (see Rule 226).

In stationary queues of traffic, drivers should apply the parking brake and, once the following traffic has stopped, take their foot off the footbrake to deactivate the vehicle brake lights. This will minimise glare to road users behind until the traffic moves again.

Law RVLR reg 27

You should also

- use dipped headlights, or dim-dip if fitted, at night in built-up areas and in dull daytime weather, to ensure that you can be seen

- keep your headlights dipped when overtaking until you are level with the other vehicle and then change to main beam if necessary, unless this would dazzle oncoming road users

- slow down, and if necessary stop, if you are dazzled by oncoming headlights.

116 **Hazard warning lights.** These may be used when your vehicle is stationary, to warn that it is temporarily obstructing traffic. Never use them as an excuse for dangerous or illegal parking. You **MUST NOT** use hazard warning lights while driving or being towed unless you are on a motorway or unrestricted dual carriageway and you need to warn drivers behind you of a hazard or obstruction ahead. Only use them for long enough to ensure that your warning has been observed.

Law RVLR reg 27

Control of the vehicle

Braking

117 **In normal circumstances.** The safest way to brake is to do so early and lightly. Brake more firmly as you begin to stop. Ease the pressure off just before the vehicle comes to rest to avoid a jerky stop.

118 **In an emergency.** Brake immediately. Try to avoid braking so harshly that you lock your wheels. Locked wheels can lead to loss of control.

119 **Skids.** Skidding is usually caused by the driver braking, accelerating or steering too harshly or driving too fast for the road conditions. If skidding occurs, remove the cause by releasing the brake pedal fully or easing off the accelerator. Turn the steering wheel in the direction of the skid. For example, if the rear of the vehicle skids to the right, steer immediately to the right to recover.

Rule 119
Rear of the car skids to the right. Driver steers to the right

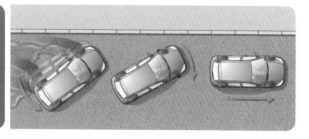

120 **ABS.** If your vehicle is fitted with anti-lock brakes, you should follow the advice given in the vehicle handbook. However, in the case of an emergency, apply the footbrake firmly; do not release the pressure until the vehicle has slowed to the desired speed. The ABS should ensure that steering control will be retained, but do not assume that a vehicle with ABS will stop in a shorter distance.

121 **Brakes affected by water.** If you have driven through deep water your brakes may be less effective. Test them at the first safe opportunity by pushing gently on the brake pedal to make sure that they work. If they are not fully effective, gently apply light pressure while driving slowly. This will help to dry them out.

122 **Coasting.** This term describes a vehicle travelling in neutral or with the clutch pressed down. It can reduce driver control because

- engine braking is eliminated

- vehicle speed downhill will increase quickly

- increased use of the footbrake can reduce its effectiveness

- steering response will be affected, particularly on bends and corners

- it may be more difficult to select the appropriate gear when needed.

123 **The driver and the environment.** You **MUST NOT** leave a parked vehicle unattended with the engine running or leave a vehicle engine running unnecessarily while that vehicle is stationary on a public road. Generally, if the vehicle is stationary and is likely to remain so for more than a couple of minutes, you should apply the parking brake and switch off the engine to reduce emissions and noise pollution. However it is permissible to leave the engine running if the vehicle is stationary in traffic or for diagnosing faults.

Law CUR regs 98 & 107

Speed limits

Type of vehicle	Built-up areas mph (km/h)	Single carriage-ways mph (km/h)	Dual carriage-ways mph (km/h)	Motorways mph (km/h)
Cars & motorcycles (including car-derived vans up to 2 tonnes maximum laden weight)	30 (48)	60 (96)	70 (112)	70 (112)
Cars towing caravans or trailers (including car-derived vans and motorcycles)	30 (48)	50 (80)	60 (96)	60 (96)
Motorhomes or motor caravans (not exceeding 3.05 tonnes maximum unladen weight)	30 (48)	60 (96)	70 (112)	70 (112)
Motorhomes or motor caravans (exceeding 3.05 tonnes maximum unladen weight)	30 (48)	50 (80)	60 (96)	70 (112)
Buses, coaches and minibuses (not exceeding 12 metres in overall length)	30 (48)	50 (80)	60 (96)	70[†] (112)
Goods vehicles (not exceeding 7.5 tonnes maximum laden weight)	30 (48)	50 (80)	60 (96)	70[††] (112)
Goods vehicles (exceeding 7.5 tonnes maximum laden weight) in England and Wales	30 (48)	50 (80)	60 (96)	60 (96)
Goods vehicles (exceeding 7.5 tonnes maximum laden weight) in Scotland	30 (48)	40 (64)	50 (80)	60 (96)

[†] 60 mph (96 km/h) if exceeding 12 metres in overall length.
[††] 60 mph (96 km/h) if articulated or towing a trailer.

For speed limits that apply to special types of vehicles, such as oversized vehicles, see Further reading.

Speed limits

124 You **MUST NOT** exceed the maximum speed limits for the road and for your vehicle (see the Speed limits table on the previous page). A speed limit of 30 mph (48 km/h) generally applies to all roads with street lights (excluding motorways) unless signs show otherwise.

Locally set speed limits may apply, for example

- 20 mph (32 km/h) in some built-up areas
- 50 mph (80 km/h) on single carriageways with known hazards
- variable speed limit signs are used on some motorways and dual carriageways to change the maximum speed limit.

Speed limits are enforced by the police.

Law RTRA sects 81, 86, 89 & sched 6 as amended by MV(VSL)(E&W)

Rule 124
Examples of speed enforcement

125 The speed limit is the absolute maximum and does not mean it is safe to drive at that speed irrespective of conditions. Unsafe speed increases the chances of causing a collision (or being unable to avoid one), as well as its severity. Inappropriate speeds are also intimidating, deterring people from walking, cycling or riding horses. Driving at speeds too fast for the road and traffic conditions is dangerous. You should always reduce your speed when

- the road layout or condition presents hazards, such as bends
- sharing the road with pedestrians, particularly children, older adults or disabled people, cyclists and horse riders, horse-drawn vehicles and motorcyclists
- weather conditions make it safer to do so
- driving at night as it is more difficult to see other road users.

49

126 **Stopping distances.** Drive at a speed that will allow you to stop well within the distance you can see to be clear. You should

- leave enough space between you and the vehicle in front so that you can pull up safely if it suddenly slows down or stops. The safe rule is never to get closer than the overall stopping distance (see Typical Stopping Distances diagram, shown over the page)

- allow at least a two-second gap between you and the vehicle in front on high-speed roads and in tunnels where visibility is reduced. The gap should be at least doubled on wet roads and up to ten times greater on icy roads

- remember, large vehicles and motorcycles need a greater distance to stop. If driving a large vehicle in a tunnel, you should allow a four-second gap between you and the vehicle in front.

If you have to stop in a tunnel, leave at least a 5-metre gap between you and the vehicle in front.

Rule 126
Use a fixed point, such as a sign, to help measure a two-second gap

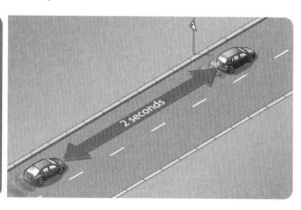

Tailgating is where the gap between you and the vehicle in front is too small for you to be able to stop safely if the vehicle in front suddenly brakes.

Tailgating is dangerous, intimidating and can cause collisions, especially when driving at speed. Keeping a safe distance from the vehicle in front gives you time to react and stop if necessary. Dangerous and careless driving offences, such as tailgating, are enforced by the police.

Lines and lane markings on the road

Diagrams of all lines are shown in Road markings.

127 **A broken white line.** This marks the centre of the road. When this line lengthens and the gaps shorten, it means that there is a hazard ahead. Do not cross it unless you can see the road is clear and wish to overtake or turn off.

128 **Double white lines where the line nearest to you is broken.** This means you may cross the lines to overtake if it is safe, provided you can complete the manoeuvre before reaching a solid white line on your side. White direction arrows on the road indicate that you need to get back onto your side of the road.

129 **Double white lines where the line nearest you is solid.** This means you **MUST NOT** cross or straddle it unless it is safe and you need to enter adjoining premises or a side road. You may cross the line if necessary, provided the road is clear, to pass a stationary vehicle, or overtake a pedal cycle, horse or road maintenance vehicle, if they are travelling at 10 mph (16 km/h) or less.
Laws RTA 1988 sect 36 & TSRGD schedule 9 part 8

130 **Areas of white diagonal stripes** or chevrons painted on the road. These are to separate traffic lanes or to protect traffic turning right.

- If the area is bordered by a broken white line, you should not enter the area unless it is necessary and you can see that it is safe to do so.

- If the area is marked with chevrons and bordered by solid white lines you **MUST NOT** enter it except in an emergency.
Laws MT(E&W)R regs 5, 9, 10 & 16, MT(S)R regs 4, 8, 9 & 14, RTA 1988 sect 36 & TSRGD schedule 9 part 8

131 **Lane dividers.** These are short, broken white lines which are used on wide carriageways to divide them into lanes. You should keep between them.

Typical stopping distances

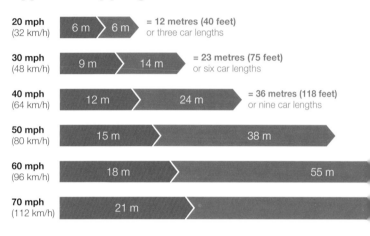

20 mph (32 km/h)	6 m / 6 m	**= 12 metres (40 feet)** or three car lengths
30 mph (48 km/h)	9 m / 14 m	**= 23 metres (75 feet)** or six car lengths
40 mph (64 km/h)	12 m / 24 m	**= 36 metres (118 feet)** or nine car lengths
50 mph (80 km/h)	15 m / 38 m	
60 mph (96 km/h)	18 m / 55 m	
70 mph (112 km/h)	21 m /	

132

Reflective road studs may be used with white lines.

- White studs mark the lanes or the middle of the road.

- Red studs mark the left edge of the road.

- Amber studs mark the central reservation of a dual carriageway or motorway.

- Green studs mark the edge of the main carriageway at lay-bys and slip roads.

- Green/yellow studs indicate temporary adjustments to lane layouts, e.g. where road works are taking place.

Rule 132
Reflective road studs mark the lanes and edges of the carriageway

The distances shown are a general guide. The distance will depend on your attention (thinking distance), the road surface, the weather conditions and the condition of your vehicle at the time.

Thinking Distance	Braking Distance

Average car length = 4 metres (13 feet)

= 53 metres (175 feet)
or thirteen car lengths

= 73 metres (240 feet)
or eighteen car lengths

75 m
= 96 metres (315 feet)
or twenty-four car lengths

Multi-lane carriageways

Lane discipline

133 If you need to change lane, first use your mirrors and if necessary take a quick sideways glance to make sure you will not force another road user to change course or speed. When it is safe to do so, signal to indicate your intentions to other road users and when clear, move over.

134 You should follow the signs and road markings and get into the lane as directed. In congested road conditions do not change lanes unnecessarily. Merging in turn is recommended but only if safe and appropriate when vehicles are travelling at a very low speed, e.g. when approaching road works or a road traffic incident. It is not recommended at high speed.

Single carriageway

135 Where a single carriageway has three lanes and the road markings or signs do not give priority to traffic in either direction

- use the middle lane only for overtaking or turning right. Remember, you have no more right to use the middle lane than a driver coming from the opposite direction

- do not use the right-hand lane.

136 Where a single carriageway has four or more lanes, use only the lanes that signs or markings indicate.

Dual carriageways
A dual carriageway is a road which has a central reservation to separate the carriageways.

137 On a two-lane dual carriageway you should stay in the left-hand lane. Use the right-hand lane for overtaking or turning right. After overtaking, move back to the left-hand lane when it is safe to do so.

138 On a dual carriageway with three or more lanes, you may use the middle lanes or the right-hand lane to overtake but you should return to the middle lanes and then the left-hand lane when it is safe to do so.

139 **Climbing and crawler lanes.** These are provided on some hills. Use this lane if you are driving a slow-moving vehicle or if there are vehicles behind you wishing to overtake. Be aware of the signs and road markings which indicate the lane is about to end.

140 **Cycle lanes and cycle tracks.** Cycle lanes are shown by road markings and signs. You **MUST NOT** drive or park in a cycle lane marked by a solid white line during its times of operation. Do not drive or park in a cycle lane marked by a broken white line unless it is unavoidable. You **MUST NOT** park in any cycle lane whilst waiting restrictions apply.

You should give way to any cyclists in a cycle lane, including when they are approaching from behind you – do not cut across them when you are turning or when you are changing lane (see Rule H3). Be prepared to stop and wait for a safe gap in the flow of cyclists before crossing the cycle lane.

Cycle tracks are routes for cyclists that are physically protected or located away from motor traffic, other than where they cross side roads. Cycle tracks may be shared with pedestrians.

You should give way to cyclists approaching or using the cycle track when you are turning into or out of a junction (see Rule H3). Be prepared to stop and wait for a safe gap in the flow of cyclists before crossing the cycle track, which may be used by cyclists travelling in both directions.

Bear in mind that cyclists are not obliged to use cycle lanes or cycle tracks.

Law RTRA sects 5 & 8

141 **Bus lanes.** These are shown by road markings and signs that indicate which (if any) other vehicles are permitted to use the bus lane. Unless otherwise indicated, you should not drive in a bus lane during its period of operation. You may enter a bus lane to stop, to load or unload where this is not prohibited.

142 **High-occupancy vehicle lanes and other designated vehicle lanes.** Lanes may be restricted for use by particular types of vehicle; these restrictions may apply some or all of the time. The operating times and vehicle types will be indicated on the accompanying traffic signs. You **MUST NOT** drive in such lanes during their times of operation unless signs indicate that your vehicle is permitted (see Traffic signs).

Vehicles permitted to use designated lanes may or may not include cycles, buses, taxis, licensed private hire vehicles, motorcycles, heavy goods vehicles (HGVs) and high-occupancy vehicles (HOVs).

Where HOV lanes are in operation, they **MUST ONLY** be used by

- vehicles containing at least the minimum number of people indicated on the traffic signs
- any other vehicles, such as buses and motorcycles, as indicated on signs prior to the start of the lane, irrespective of the number of occupants.

Laws RTRA sects 5 & 8, & RTA 1988 sect 36

143 **One-way streets.** Traffic **MUST** travel in the direction indicated by signs. Buses and/or cycles may have a contraflow lane. Choose the correct lane for your exit as soon as you can. Do not change lanes suddenly. Unless road signs or markings indicate otherwise, you should use

- the left-hand lane when going left
- the right-hand lane when going right
- the most appropriate lane when going straight ahead. Remember – traffic could be passing on both sides.

Laws RTA 1988 sect 36 & RTRA sects 5 & 8

General advice

144 You **MUST NOT**

- drive dangerously
- drive without due care and attention
- drive without reasonable consideration for other road users.

Driving requires focus and attention at all times. Remember, you may be driving dangerously or travelling too fast even if you don't mean to.

Law RTA 1988 sects 2 & 3 as amended by RTA 1991

145 You **MUST NOT** drive on or over a pavement, footpath or bridleway except to gain lawful access to property, or in the case of an emergency.

Laws HA 1835 sect 72 & RTA 1988 sect 34

146 **Adapt your driving** to the appropriate type and condition of road you are on. In particular

- do not treat speed limits as a target. It is often not appropriate or safe to drive at the maximum speed limit
- take the road and traffic conditions into account. Be prepared for unexpected or difficult situations, for example, the road being blocked beyond a blind bend. Be prepared to adjust your speed as a precaution

- where there are junctions, be prepared for road users emerging

- in side roads and country lanes look out for unmarked junctions where nobody has priority

- be prepared to stop at traffic control systems, road works, pedestrian crossings or traffic lights as necessary

- try to anticipate what pedestrians and cyclists might do. If pedestrians, particularly children, are looking the other way, they may step out into the road without seeing you.

147
Be considerate. Be careful of and considerate towards all types of road users, especially those requiring extra care (see Rule 204).

- You **MUST NOT** throw anything out of a vehicle; for example, food or food packaging, cigarette ends, cans, paper or carrier bags. This can endanger other road users, particularly motorcyclists and cyclists.

- Try to be understanding if other road users cause problems; they may be inexperienced or not know the area well.

- Be patient; remember that anyone can make a mistake.

- Do not allow yourself to become agitated or involved if someone is behaving badly on the road. This will only make the situation worse. Pull over, calm down and, when you feel relaxed, continue your journey.

- Slow down and hold back if a road user pulls out into your path at a junction. Allow them to get clear. Do not over-react by driving too close behind to intimidate them.

Law EPA sect 87

148
Safe driving and riding needs concentration.
Avoid distractions when driving or riding such as

- loud music (this may mask other sounds)
- trying to read maps
- starting or adjusting any music or radio
- arguing with your passengers or other road users
- eating and drinking
- smoking.

You **MUST NOT** smoke in public transport vehicles or in vehicles used for work purposes in certain prescribed circumstances. Separate regulations apply to England, Wales and Scotland. In England and Wales, the driver must not smoke or allow anyone to smoke in an enclosed private vehicle carrying someone under 18, including motor caravans. In Scotland it is an offence for anyone aged 18 or over to smoke in a private motor vehicle (unless it is parked and being used as living accommodation) when there is someone under 18 in the vehicle and the vehicle is in a public place.

Laws TSf(EV)R, TSfP(W)R, TPSCP(S)R, S-f(PV)R, S-f(W)R & SP(CIMV)(S)A

Mobile phones and in-vehicle technology

You **MUST** exercise proper control of your vehicle at all times. You **MUST NOT** use a hand-held mobile phone, or similar device, capable of interactive communication (such as a tablet) for any purpose when driving or when supervising a learner driver. This ban covers all use of a hand-held interactive communication device and it applies even when the interactive communication capability is turned off or unavailable. You **MUST NOT** pick up the phone or similar device while driving to dial a number and then put it in the cradle for the duration of the conversation. You **MUST NOT** pick up and use your hand-held phone or similar device while stationary in traffic.

There is an exception to call 999 or 112 in a genuine emergency when it is unsafe or impractical to stop. There is also an exception if you are using a hand-held mobile phone or similar device to make a contactless payment at a contactless payment terminal. Your vehicle **MUST** be stationary, and the goods or services received at the same time as, or after, the contactless payment.

Never use a hand-held microphone when driving. Using hands-free equipment is also likely to distract your attention from the road. It is far safer not to use any telephone or similar device while you are driving or riding – find a safe place to stop first or use the voicemail facility and listen to messages later.

You may park your vehicle using a hand-held remote control app or device. The app or device **MUST** be legal, and you should not put other people in danger when you use it.

Laws RTA 1988 sects 2 & 3, & CUR regs 104 & 110

150 There is a danger of driver distraction being caused by in-vehicle systems such as satellite navigation systems, congestion warning systems, PCs, multi-media, etc. You **MUST** exercise proper control of your vehicle at all times. Do not rely on driver assistance systems such as motorway assist, lane departure warnings, or remote control parking. They are available to assist but you should not reduce your concentration levels. Do not be distracted by maps or screen-based information (such as navigation or vehicle management systems) while driving or riding. If necessary find a safe place to stop.

As the driver, you are still responsible for the vehicle if you use a driver assistance system (like motorway assist). This is also the case if you use a hand-held remote control parking app or device. You **MUST** have full control over these systems at all times.

Laws RTA 1988 sects 2 & 3, & CUR regs 104 & 110

Rule 151
Do not block access to a side road

151 **In slow-moving traffic.** You should

- reduce the distance between you and the vehicle ahead to maintain traffic flow
- never get so close to the vehicle in front that you cannot stop safely

- leave enough space to be able to manoeuvre if the vehicle in front breaks down or an emergency vehicle needs to get past
- not change lanes to the left to overtake
- allow access into and from side roads, as blocking these will add to congestion
- allow pedestrians and cyclists to cross in front of you
- be aware of cyclists and motorcyclists who may be passing on either side.

Driving in built-up areas

Residential streets. You should drive slowly and carefully on streets where there are likely to be pedestrians, cyclists and parked cars. In some areas a 20 mph (32 km/h) maximum speed limit may be in force. Look out for

- vehicles emerging from junctions or driveways
- vehicles moving off
- car doors opening
- pedestrians
- children running out from between parked cars
- cyclists and motorcyclists.

Traffic-calming measures. On some roads there are features such as road humps, chicanes and narrowings which are intended to slow you down. When you approach these features reduce your speed. Allow cyclists and motorcyclists room to pass through them. Maintain a reduced speed along the whole of the stretch of road within the calming measures. Give way to oncoming road users if directed to do so by signs. You should not overtake other moving road users while in these areas.

Rule 153 Chicanes may be used to slow traffic down

Country roads

154 Take extra care on country roads and reduce your speed at approaches to bends, which can be sharper than they appear, and at junctions and turnings, which may be partially hidden. Be prepared for pedestrians, horse riders, cyclists, slow-moving farm vehicles or mud on the road surface. Make sure you can stop within the distance you can see to be clear. You should also reduce your speed where country roads enter villages.

155 **Single-track roads.** These are only wide enough for one vehicle. They may have special passing places. If you see a vehicle coming towards you, or the driver behind wants to overtake, pull into a passing place on your left, or wait opposite a passing place on your right. Give way to road users coming uphill whenever you can. If necessary, reverse until you reach a passing place to let the other vehicle pass. Slow down when passing pedestrians, cyclists and horse riders.

156 Do not park in passing places.

Vehicles prohibited from using roads and pavements

157 Certain motorised vehicles do not meet the construction and technical requirements for road vehicles and are generally not intended, not suitable and not legal for road, pavement, footpath, cycle path or bridleway use. These include most types of miniature motorcycles, also called mini motos, and motorised scooters, also called go peds, which are powered by electric or internal combustion engines. These types of vehicle **MUST NOT** be used on roads, pavements, footpaths or bridleways.

Laws RTA 1988 sects 34, 41a, 42, 47, 63 & 66, HA 1835 sect 72 & R(S)A sect 129

158 Certain models of motorcycles, motor tricycles and quadricycles, also called quad bikes, are suitable only for off-road use and do not meet legal standards for use on roads. Vehicles that do not meet these standards **MUST NOT** be used on roads. They **MUST NOT** be used on pavements, footpaths, cycle paths or bridleways either. You **MUST** make sure that any motorcycle, motor tricycle, quadricycle or any other motor vehicle meets legal standards and is properly registered, taxed and insured before using it on the roads. Even when registered, taxed and insured for the road, vehicles **MUST NOT** be used on pavements.

Laws RTA 1988 sects 34, 41a, 42, 47, 63, 66 & 156, HA 1835 sect 72, R(S)A sect 129 & VERA sects 1, 29, 31A & 43A

Using the road

General rules

159 Before moving off you should

- use all mirrors to check the road is clear

- look round to check the blind spots (the areas you are unable to see in the mirrors)

- signal if necessary before moving out

- look round for a final check.

Move off only when it is safe to do so.

Rule 159
Check the blind spot before moving off

Once moving you should

- keep to the left, unless road signs or markings indicate otherwise. The exceptions are when you want to overtake, turn right or pass parked vehicles or pedestrians in the road

- keep well to the left on right-hand bends. This will improve your view of the road and help avoid the risk of colliding with traffic approaching from the opposite direction

- drive or ride with both hands on the wheel or handlebars where possible. This will help you to remain in full control of the vehicle at all times. You may use driver assistance systems while you are driving. Make sure you use any system according to the manufacturer's instructions

- be aware of other road users, especially cycles and motorcycles who may be filtering through the traffic. These are more difficult to see than larger vehicles and their riders are particularly vulnerable. Give them plenty of room, especially if you are driving a long vehicle or towing a trailer. You should give way to cyclists when you are changing direction or lane – do not cut across them

- select a lower gear before you reach a long downhill slope. This will help to control your speed

- when towing, remember the extra length will affect overtaking and manoeuvring. The extra weight will also affect the braking and acceleration.

Mirrors. All mirrors should be used effectively throughout your journey. You should

- use your mirrors frequently so that you always know what is behind and to each side of you

- use them in good time before you signal or change direction or speed

- be aware that mirrors do not cover all areas and there will be blind spots. You will need to look round and check.

Remember: Mirrors – Signal – Manoeuvre

Overtaking

Before overtaking you should make sure

- the road is sufficiently clear ahead

- road users are not beginning to overtake you

- there is a suitable gap in front of the road user you plan to overtake.

Overtake only when it is safe and legal to do so. You should

- not get too close to the vehicle you intend to overtake

- use your mirrors, signal when it is safe to do so, take a quick sideways glance, if necessary, into the blind spot area and then start to move out

- not assume that you can simply follow a vehicle ahead which is overtaking; there may only be enough room for one vehicle

- move quickly past the vehicle you are overtaking, once you have started to overtake. Allow plenty of room. Move back to the left as soon as you can but do not cut in

- take extra care at night and in poor visibility when it is harder to judge speed and distance

- give way to oncoming vehicles before passing parked vehicles or other obstructions on your side of the road

- only overtake on the left if the vehicle in front is signalling to turn right, and there is room to do so

- stay in your lane if traffic is moving slowly in queues. If the queue on your right is moving more slowly than you are, you may pass on the left. Cyclists may pass slower moving or stationary traffic on their right or left, and should proceed with caution as the driver may not be able to see you. Be careful about doing so, particularly on the approach to junctions, and especially when deciding whether it is safe to pass lorries or other large vehicles.

- give motorcyclists, cyclists, horse riders and horse-drawn vehicles at least as much room as you would when overtaking a car (see Rules 211–215). As a guide

- leave at least 1.5 metres when overtaking cyclists at speeds of up to 30 mph, and give them more space when overtaking at higher speeds

- pass horse riders and horse-drawn vehicles at speeds under 10 mph and allow at least 2 metres of space

- allow at least 2 metres of space and keep to a low speed when passing a pedestrian who is walking in the road (for example, where there is no pavement)

- take extra care and give more space when overtaking motorcyclists, cyclists, horse riders, horse-drawn vehicles and pedestrians in bad weather (including high winds) and at night

- you should wait behind the motorcyclist, cyclist, horse rider, horse-drawn vehicle or pedestrian and not overtake if it is unsafe or not possible to meet these clearances.

Remember: Mirrors – Signal – Manoeuvre

Rule 163
Give vulnerable road users at least as much space as you would a car

 Large vehicles. Overtaking these is more difficult. You should

- drop back. This will increase your ability to see ahead and should allow the driver of the large vehicle to see you in their mirrors. Getting too close to large vehicles, including agricultural vehicles such as a tractor with a trailer or other fixed equipment, will obscure your view of the road ahead and there may be another slow-moving vehicle in front

- make sure that you have enough room to complete your overtaking manoeuvre before committing yourself. It takes longer to pass a large vehicle. If in doubt do not overtake

- not assume you can follow a vehicle ahead which is overtaking a long vehicle. If a problem develops, they may abort overtaking and pull back in.

 You **MUST NOT** overtake

- if you would have to cross or straddle double white lines with a solid line nearest to you (but see Rule 129)

- if you would have to enter an area designed to divide traffic, if it is surrounded by a solid white line

- the nearest vehicle to a pedestrian crossing, especially when it has stopped to let pedestrians cross

- if you would have to enter a lane reserved for buses, trams or cycles during its hours of operation

- after a 'No Overtaking' sign and until you pass a sign cancelling the restriction.

Laws RTA 1988 sect 36 & TSRGD schedule 1, schedule 9 part 7, schedule 14 part 1

 DO NOT overtake if there is any doubt, or where you cannot see far enough ahead to be sure it is safe. For example, when you are approaching

- a corner or bend

- a hump bridge
- the brow of a hill.

 DO NOT overtake where you might come into conflict with other road users. For example

- approaching or at a road junction on either side of the road
- where the road narrows
- when approaching a school crossing patrol
- on the approach to crossing facilities
- where a vehicle ahead is slowing to stop for a pedestrian that is crossing from a pedestrian island (see Rule 165)
- between the kerb and a bus or tram when it is at a stop
- where traffic is queuing at junctions or road works
- when you would force another road user to swerve or slow down
- at a level crossing
- when a road user is indicating right, even if you believe the signal should have been cancelled. Do not take a risk; wait for the signal to be cancelled
- stay behind if you are following a cyclist approaching a roundabout or junction, and you intend to turn left. Do not cut across cyclists going ahead, including those using cycle lanes and cycle tracks (see Rule H3)
- stay behind if you are following a horse rider or horse-drawn vehicle approaching a roundabout or junction and you intend to turn left. Do not cut across a horse rider or horse-drawn vehicle going ahead
- when a tram is standing at a kerbside tram stop and there is no clearly marked passing lane for other traffic.

 Being overtaken. If a driver is trying to overtake you, maintain a steady course and speed, slowing down if necessary to let the vehicle pass. Never obstruct drivers who wish to pass. Speeding up or driving unpredictably while someone is overtaking you is dangerous. Drop back to maintain a two-second gap if someone overtakes and pulls into the gap in front of you.

169 Do not hold up a long queue of traffic, especially if you are driving a large or slow-moving vehicle. Check your mirrors frequently, and if necessary, pull in where it is safe and let traffic pass.

Road junctions

170 Take extra care at junctions. You should

- watch out for cyclists, motorcyclists and pedestrians, including powered wheelchair/mobility scooter users, as they are not always easy to see. Be aware that they may not have seen or heard you if you are approaching from behind

- give way to pedestrians crossing or waiting to cross a road into which or from which you are turning. If they have started to cross, they have priority so give way (see Rule H2)

Rule 170
Give way to pedestrians who have started to cross

- remain behind cyclists, horse riders, horse-drawn vehicles and motorcyclists at junctions even if they are waiting to turn and are positioned close to the kerb

- watch out for long vehicles that may be turning at a junction ahead; they may have to use the whole width of the road to make the turn (see Rule 221)

- watch out for horse riders who may take a different line on the road from that which you would expect

- not assume, when waiting at a junction, that a vehicle coming from the right and signalling left will actually turn. Wait and make sure

- look all around before emerging. Do not cross or join a road until there is a gap large enough for you to do so safely.

171 You **MUST** stop behind the line at a junction with a 'Stop' sign and a solid white line across the road. Wait for a safe gap in the traffic before you move off.

Laws RTA 1988 sect 36 & TSRGD schedule 9 parts 7 and 8

172 The approach to a junction may have a 'Give Way' sign or a triangle marked on the road. You **MUST** give way to traffic on the main road when emerging from a junction with broken white lines across the road.

Laws RTA 1988 sect 36 & TSRGD schedule 9 parts 7 and 8

Rule 173
Assess your vehicle's length and do not obstruct traffic

173 **Dual carriageways.** When crossing or turning right, first assess whether the central reservation is deep enough to protect the full length of your vehicle.

- If it is, then you should treat each half of the carriageway as a separate road. Wait in the central reservation until there is a safe gap in the traffic on the second half of the road.

- If the central reservation is too shallow for the length of your vehicle, wait until you can cross both carriageways in one go.

Rule 174
Enter a box junction only if your exit road is clear

174 **Box junctions.** These have criss-cross yellow lines painted on the road (see Road markings). You **MUST NOT** enter the box until your exit road or lane is clear. However, you may enter the box and wait when you want to turn right, and are only stopped from doing so by oncoming traffic, or by other vehicles waiting to turn right. At signalled roundabouts you **MUST NOT** enter the box unless you can cross over it completely without stopping.

Law TSRGD schedule 9 parts 7 and 8

Junctions controlled by traffic lights

175 You **MUST** stop behind the white 'Stop' line across your side of the road unless the light is green. If the amber light appears you may go on only if you have already crossed the stop line or are so close to it that to stop might cause a collision.

Laws RTA 1988 sect 36 & TSRGD schedule 14 parts 1 and 4

176 You **MUST NOT** move forward over the white line when the red light is showing. Only go forward when the traffic lights are green if there is room for you to clear the junction safely or you are taking up a position to turn right. If the traffic lights are not working, treat the situation as you would an unmarked junction and proceed with great care.

Laws RTA 1988 sect 36 & TSRGD schedule 14 parts 1 and 4

 Green filter arrow. This indicates a filter lane only. Do not enter that lane unless you want to go in the direction of the arrow. You may proceed in the direction of the green arrow when it, or the full green light shows. Give other traffic, especially cyclists, time and room to move into the correct lane.

Rule 178
Do not unnecessarily encroach on the cyclists' waiting area

 Advanced stop lines. Some signal-controlled junctions have advanced stop lines to allow cyclists to be positioned ahead of other traffic. Motorists, including motorcyclists, **MUST** stop at the first white line reached if the lights are amber or red and should avoid blocking the way or encroaching on the marked area at other times; for example, if the junction ahead is blocked. If your vehicle has proceeded over the first white line at the time that the signal goes red, you should stop as soon as possible and **MUST** stop at the second white line. Allow cyclists, including any moving or waiting alongside you, enough time and space to move off when the green signal shows.

Drivers of large vehicles should stop sufficiently far behind the first white line so that they can see the whole area where cyclists may be waiting, allowing for any blind spot in front of the vehicle.

Laws RTA 1988 sect 36 & TSRGD schedule 14 part 1

Turning right

Well before you turn right you should

- use your mirrors to make sure you know the position and movement of traffic behind you

- give a right-turn signal

- take up a position just left of the middle of the road or in the space marked for traffic turning right

- leave room for other vehicles to pass on the left, if possible.

Wait until there is a safe gap between you and any oncoming vehicle. Watch out for cyclists, motorcyclists, pedestrians and other road users. Check your mirrors and blind spot again to make sure you are not being overtaken, then make the turn. Do not cut the corner. Take great care when turning into a main road; you will need to watch for traffic in both directions and wait for a safe gap.

Remember: Mirrors – Signal – Manoeuvre

Rule 180
Position your vehicle correctly to avoid obstructing traffic

When turning right at crossroads where an oncoming vehicle is also turning right, there is a choice of two methods

- turn right side to right side; keep the other vehicle on your right and turn behind it. This is generally the safer method as you have a clear view of any approaching traffic when completing your turn

- left side to left side, turning in front of each other. This can block your view of oncoming vehicles, so take extra care. Cyclists and motorcyclists in particular may be hidden from your view. Road layout, markings or how the other vehicle is positioned can determine which course should be taken.

Rule 181
Left – Turning right side to right side.
Right – Turning left side to left side

Turning left

182 Use your mirrors and give a left-turn signal well before you turn left. Do not overtake just before you turn left and watch out for traffic coming up on your left before you make the turn, especially if driving a large vehicle. Cyclists, motorcyclists and other road users in particular may be hidden from your view.

Rule 182
Do not cut in on cyclists

183 When turning

- keep as close to the left as is safe and practicable

- give way to any vehicles using a bus lane, cycle lane, cycle track or tramway from either direction, including when they are passing slow-moving or stationary vehicles on either side.

Roundabouts

184 **On approaching a roundabout** take notice and act on all the information available to you, including traffic signs, traffic lights and lane markings which direct you into the correct lane. You should

- use **Mirrors – Signal – Manoeuvre** at all stages

- decide as early as possible which exit you need to take

- give an appropriate signal (see Rule 186). Time your signals so as not to confuse other road users

- get into the correct lane

- adjust your speed and position to fit in with traffic conditions

- be aware of the speed and position of all the road users around you.

When reaching the roundabout you should

- give priority to traffic approaching from your right, unless directed otherwise by signs, road markings or traffic lights

- check whether road markings allow you to enter the roundabout without giving way. If so, proceed, but still look to the right before joining

- watch out for all other road users already on the roundabout; be aware they may not be signalling correctly or at all

- look forward before moving off to make sure traffic in front has moved off.

Rule 185
Follow the correct procedure at roundabouts

Signals and position. When taking the first exit to the left, unless signs or markings indicate otherwise

- signal left and approach in the left-hand lane

- keep to the left on the roundabout and continue signalling left to leave.

When taking an exit to the right or going full circle, unless signs or markings indicate otherwise

- signal right and approach in the right-hand lane
- keep to the right on the roundabout until you need to change lanes to exit the roundabout
- signal left after you have passed the exit before the one you want.

When taking any intermediate exit, unless signs or markings indicate otherwise

- select the appropriate lane on approach to the roundabout
- you should not normally need to signal on approach
- stay in this lane until you need to alter course to exit the roundabout
- signal left after you have passed the exit before the one you want.

When there are more than three lanes at the entrance to a roundabout, use the most appropriate lane on approach and through it.

You should give priority to cyclists on the roundabout. They will be travelling more slowly than motorised traffic. Give them plenty of room and do not attempt to overtake them within their lane. Allow them to move across your path as they travel around the roundabout.

Cyclists, horse riders and horse-drawn vehicles may stay in the left-hand lane when they intend to continue across or around the roundabout and should signal right to show you they are not leaving the roundabout. Drivers should take extra care when entering a roundabout to ensure that they do not cut across cyclists, horse riders or horse-drawn vehicles in the left-hand lane, who are continuing around the roundabout.

In all cases watch out for and give plenty of room to

- pedestrians who may be crossing the approach and exit roads
- traffic crossing in front of you on the roundabout, especially vehicles intending to leave by the next exit

- traffic which may be straddling lanes or positioned incorrectly
- motorcyclists
- long vehicles (including those towing trailers). These might have to take a different course or straddle lanes either approaching or on the roundabout because of their length. Watch out for their signals.

188 **Mini-roundabouts.** Approach these in the same way as normal roundabouts. All vehicles **MUST** pass round the central markings except large vehicles which are physically incapable of doing so. Remember, there is less space to manoeuvre and less time to signal. Avoid making U-turns at mini-roundabouts. Beware of others doing this.

Laws RTA 1988 sect 36 & TSRGD schedule 9 parts 7 and 8

189 At double mini-roundabouts treat each roundabout separately and give way to traffic from the right.

190 **Multiple roundabouts.** At some complex junctions, there may be a series of mini-roundabouts at each intersection. Treat each mini-roundabout separately and follow the normal rules.

Rule 190
Treat each roundabout separately

Pedestrian crossings

191 You **MUST NOT** park on a crossing or in the area covered by the zig-zag lines. You **MUST NOT** overtake the moving vehicle nearest the crossing or the vehicle nearest the crossing which has stopped to give way to pedestrians.

Laws RTRA sect 25(5) & TSRGD schedule 14 parts 1 and 5

192 In slow-moving and queuing traffic, you should keep crossings completely clear, as blocking these makes it difficult and dangerous for pedestrians to cross. You should not enter a pedestrian crossing if you are unable to completely clear the crossing. Nor should you block advanced stop lines for cycles.

Rule 192
Keep the crossing clear

193 You should take extra care where the view of either side of the crossing is blocked by queuing traffic or incorrectly parked vehicles. Pedestrians may be crossing between stationary vehicles.

194 Allow pedestrians plenty of time to cross and do not harass them by revving your engine or edging forward.

195 **Zebra and parallel crossings.** As you approach a zebra crossing

- look out for pedestrians waiting to cross and be ready to slow down or stop
- you should give way to pedestrians waiting to cross
- you **MUST** give way when a pedestrian has moved onto a crossing
- allow more time for stopping on wet or icy roads
- do not wave, flash your lights or use your horn to invite pedestrians across; this could be dangerous if another vehicle is approaching
- be patient, do not sound your horn or rev your engine as this can be intimidating

- be aware of pedestrians approaching from the side of the crossing.

A zebra crossing with a central island is two separate crossings (see Rules 19 and 20).

Parallel crossings are similar to zebra crossings, but include a cycle route alongside the black and white stripes.

As you approach a parallel crossing

- look out for pedestrians or cyclists waiting to cross and slow down or stop

- you should give way to pedestrians or cyclists waiting to cross

- you **MUST** give way when a pedestrian or cyclist has moved onto a crossing

- allow more time for stopping on wet or icy roads

- do not wave, flash your lights or use your horn to invite pedestrians or cyclists across; this could be dangerous if another vehicle is approaching

- be patient, do not sound your horn or rev your engine as this can be intimidating

- be aware of pedestrians or cyclists approaching from the side of the crossing.

A parallel crossing with a central island is two separate crossings (see Rules 19 and 20).

Law TSRGD schedule 14 parts 1 and 5

Signal-controlled crossings

196 **Pelican crossings.** These are signal-controlled crossings where flashing amber follows the red 'Stop' light. You **MUST** stop when the red light shows. When the amber light is flashing, you **MUST** give way to any pedestrians on the crossing. If the amber light is flashing and there are no pedestrians on the crossing, you may proceed with caution.

Laws TSRGD reg 14 & RTRA sect 25(5)

197 Pelican crossings which go straight across the road are one crossing, even when there is a central island. You **MUST** wait for pedestrians who are crossing from the other side of the island.

Law TSRGD reg 14

198 Give way to anyone still crossing after the signal for vehicles has changed to green. This advice applies to all crossings.

199 **Toucan, puffin and equestrian crossings.** These are similar to pelican crossings, but there is no flashing amber phase; the light sequence for traffic at these three crossings is the same as at traffic lights. If the signal-controlled crossing is not working, proceed with extreme caution. Do not enter the crossing if you are unable to completely clear it, to avoid obstructing pedestrians, cyclists or horse riders.

Reversing

200 Choose an appropriate place to manoeuvre. If you need to turn your vehicle around, wait until you find a safe place. Try not to reverse or turn round in a busy road; find a quiet side road or drive round a block of side streets.

201 Do not reverse from a side road into a main road. When using a driveway, reverse in and drive out if you can.

202 Look carefully before you start reversing. You should

- use all your mirrors
- check the 'blind spot' behind you (the part of the road you cannot see easily in the mirrors)
- check there are no pedestrians (particularly children), cyclists, other road users or obstructions in the road behind you.

Reverse slowly while

- checking all around
- looking mainly through the rear window
- being aware that the front of your vehicle will swing out as you turn.

Get someone to guide you if you cannot see clearly.

Rule 202
Check all round when reversing

 203 You **MUST NOT** reverse your vehicle further than necessary.
Law CUR reg 106

Road users requiring extra care

204 The road users most at risk from road traffic are pedestrians, in particular children, older adults and disabled people, cyclists, horse riders and motorcyclists. It is particularly important to be aware of children, older adults and disabled people, and learner and inexperienced drivers and riders. In any interaction between road users, those who can cause the greatest harm have the greatest responsibility to reduce the danger or threat they pose to others.

Pedestrians

205 There is a risk of pedestrians, especially children, stepping unexpectedly into the road. You should drive with the safety of children in mind at a speed suitable for the conditions.

206 **Drive carefully and slowly** when

- in crowded shopping streets, Home Zones and Quiet Lanes (see Rule 218) or residential areas

- driving past bus and tram stops; pedestrians may emerge suddenly into the road

- passing parked vehicles, especially ice cream vans; children are more interested in ice cream than traffic and may run into the road unexpectedly

- needing to cross a pavement, cycle lane or cycle track; for example, to reach or leave a driveway or private access. Give way to pedestrians on the pavement and cyclists using a cycle lane or cycle track

- reversing into a side road; look all around the vehicle and give way to any pedestrians who may be crossing the road

- turning at road junctions; you should give way to pedestrians who are crossing or waiting to cross the road into which or from which you are turning

- going through road works or when passing roadside rescue and recovery vehicles, as there may be people working in or at the side of the road

- the pavement is closed due to street repairs and pedestrians are directed to use the road

- approaching pedestrians on narrow rural roads without a footway or footpath. Always slow down and be prepared to stop if necessary, giving them plenty of room as you drive past

- approaching zebra and parallel crossings as you **MUST** give way to pedestrians and cyclists on the crossing (see Rule 195)

- approaching pedestrians who have started to cross the road ahead of you. They have priority when crossing at a junction or side road so you should give way (see Rule H2).

Law TSRGD schedule 14 part 5

Particularly vulnerable pedestrians. These include

- children and older pedestrians who may not be able to judge your speed and could step into the road in front of you. At 40 mph (64 km/h) your vehicle will probably kill any pedestrians it hits. At 20 mph (32 km/h) there is only a 1 in 20 chance of the pedestrian being killed. So kill your speed

- older pedestrians who may need more time to cross the road. Be patient and allow them to cross in their own time. Do not hurry them by revving your engine or edging forward

- people with disabilities. People with hearing impairments may not be aware of your vehicle approaching. Those with walking difficulties require more time

- blind or partially sighted people, who may be carrying a white cane or using a guide dog. They may not be able to see you approaching

- deafblind people who may be carrying a white cane with a red band or using a dog with a red and white harness. They may not see or hear instructions or signals.

208 **Near schools.** Drive slowly and be particularly aware of young cyclists and pedestrians. In some places, there may be a flashing amber signal below the 'School' warning sign which tells you that there may be children crossing the road ahead. Drive very slowly until you are clear of the area.

209 Drive carefully and slowly when passing a stationary bus showing a 'School Bus' sign as children may be getting on or off.

210 You **MUST** stop when a school crossing patrol shows a 'Stop for children' sign (see Signals by authorised persons and Traffic signs).

Law RTRA sect 28

Motorcyclists and cyclists

211 It is often difficult to see motorcyclists and cyclists, especially when they are waiting alongside you, coming up from behind, coming out of or moving off from junctions, at roundabouts, overtaking you or filtering through traffic. Always look out for them before you emerge from a junction; they could be approaching faster than you think.

Do not turn at a junction if to do so would cause the cyclist going straight ahead to stop or swerve, just as you would do with a motor vehicle.

When turning right across a line of slow-moving or stationary traffic, look out for and give way to cyclists or motorcyclists on the inside of the traffic you are crossing. Be especially careful when moving off, turning, and when changing direction or lane. Be sure to check mirrors and blind spots carefully.

Rule 211
Look out for motorcyclists and cyclists at junctions

212 Give motorcyclists, cyclists, horse riders, horse-drawn vehicles and pedestrians walking in the road (for example, where there is no pavement), at least as much room as you would when overtaking a car (see Rules 162 to 167). Drivers should take extra care and give more space when overtaking motorcyclists, cyclists, horse riders, horse-drawn vehicles and pedestrians in bad weather (including high winds) and at night. If the rider looks over their shoulder, it could mean that they intend to pull out, turn right or change direction. Give them time and space to do so.

213 On narrow sections of road, on quiet roads or streets, at road junctions and in slower-moving traffic, cyclists may sometimes ride in the centre of the lane, rather than towards the side of the road. It can be safer for groups of cyclists to ride two abreast in these situations. Allow them to do so for their own safety, to ensure they can see and be seen. Cyclists are also advised to ride at least a door's width or 1 metre from parked cars for their own safety.

On narrow sections of road, horse riders may ride in the centre of the lane. Allow them to do so for their own safety to ensure they can see and be seen.

Motorcyclists, cyclists, horse riders and horse-drawn vehicles may suddenly need to avoid uneven road surfaces and obstacles, such as drain covers or oily, wet or icy patches on the road. Give them plenty of room and pay particular attention to any sudden change of direction they may have to make.

Other road users

214 **Animals.** When passing animals, drive slowly. Give them plenty of room and be ready to stop. Do not scare animals by sounding your horn, revving your engine or accelerating rapidly once you have passed them. Look out for animals being led, driven or ridden on the road and take extra care. Keep your speed down at bends and on narrow country roads. If a road is blocked by a herd of animals, stop and switch off your engine until they have left the road. Watch out for animals on unfenced roads.

Horse riders and horse-drawn vehicles. Be particularly careful of horse riders and horse-drawn vehicles, especially when approaching, overtaking, passing or moving away. Always pass wide and slowly. When you see a horse on a road, you should slow down to a maximum of 10 mph. Be patient, do not sound your horn or rev your engine. When safe to do so, pass wide and slow, allowing at least 2 metres of space.

Feral or semi-feral ponies found in areas such as the New Forest, Exmoor and Dartmoor require the same consideration as ridden horses when approaching or passing.

Horse riders are often children, so take extra care and remember riders may ride in double file when escorting a young or inexperienced horse or rider. Look out for horse riders' and horse drivers' signals and heed a request to slow down or stop. Take great care and treat all horses as a potential hazard; they can be unpredictable despite the efforts of their rider/driver. Remember there are three brains at work when you pass a horse; the rider's, the driver's and the horse's. Do not forget that horses are flight animals and can move incredibly quickly if startled.

 Older drivers. Their reactions may be slower than other drivers. Make allowance for this.

 Learners and inexperienced drivers. They may not be so skilful at anticipating and responding to events. Be particularly patient with learner drivers and young drivers. Drivers who have recently passed their test may display a 'New driver' plate or sticker (see Annex 8 Safety code for new drivers).

 Home Zones and Quiet Lanes. These are places where people could be using the whole of the road for a range of activities such as children playing or for a community event. You should drive slowly and carefully and be prepared to stop to allow people extra time to make space for you to pass them in safety.

Other vehicles

219 **Emergency and incident support vehicles.** You should look and listen for ambulances, fire engines, police, doctors or other emergency vehicles using flashing blue, red or green lights and sirens or flashing headlights, or traffic officer and incident support vehicles using flashing amber lights. When one approaches do not panic. Consider the route of such a vehicle and take appropriate action to let it pass, while complying with all traffic signs. If necessary, pull to the side of the road and stop, but try to avoid stopping before the brow of a hill, a bend or narrow section of road. Do not endanger yourself, other road users or pedestrians and avoid mounting the kerb. Do not brake harshly on approach to a junction or roundabout, as a following vehicle may not have the same view as you.

220 **Powered vehicles used by disabled people.** These small vehicles travel at a maximum speed of 8 mph (12 km/h). On a dual carriageway where the speed limit exceeds 50 mph (80 km/h) they **MUST** have a flashing amber beacon, but on other roads you may not have that advance warning (see Rules 36–46 inclusive).

Law RVLR regs 17(1) & 26

221 **Large vehicles.** These may need extra road space to turn or to deal with a hazard that you are not able to see. If you are following a large vehicle, such as a bus or articulated lorry, be aware that the driver may not be able to see you in the mirrors. Be prepared to stop and wait if it needs room or time to turn.

Rule 221
Large vehicles need extra room

222 Large vehicles can block your view. Your ability to see and to plan ahead will be improved if you pull back to increase your separation distance. Be patient, as larger vehicles are subject to lower speed limits than cars and motorcycles. Many large vehicles may be fitted with speed limiting devices which will restrict speed to 56 mph (90 km/h) even on a motorway.

223 **Buses, coaches and trams.** Give priority to these vehicles when you can do so safely, especially when they signal to pull away from stops. Look out for people getting off a bus or tram and crossing the road.

224 **Electric vehicles.** Be careful of electric vehicles such as milk floats and trams. Trams move quickly but silently and cannot steer to avoid you.

225 **Vehicles with flashing amber beacons.** These warn of a slow-moving or stationary vehicle (such as a traffic officer vehicle, salt spreader, snow plough or recovery vehicle) or abnormal loads, so approach with caution. On unrestricted dual carriageways, motor vehicles first used on or after 1 January 1947 with a maximum speed of 25 mph (40 km/h) or less (such as tractors) **MUST** use a flashing amber beacon (also see Rule 220).
Law RVLR reg 17

Driving in adverse weather conditions

226 You **MUST** use headlights when visibility is seriously reduced, generally when you cannot see for more than 100 metres (328 feet). You may also use front or rear fog lights but you **MUST** switch them off when visibility improves (see Rule 236).
Law RVLR regs 25 & 27

227 **Wet weather.** In wet weather, stopping distances will be at least double those required for stopping on dry roads (see the Typical stopping distances table in Rule 126). This is because your tyres have less grip on the road. In wet weather

- you should keep well back from the vehicle in front. This will increase your ability to see and plan ahead
- if the steering becomes unresponsive, it probably means that water is preventing the tyres from gripping the road. Ease off the accelerator and slow down gradually
- the rain and spray from vehicles may make it difficult to see and be seen
- be aware of the dangers of spilt diesel that will make the surface very slippery (see Annex 6)
- take extra care around pedestrians, cyclists, motorcyclists and horse riders.

Icy and snowy weather

228 In winter check the local weather forecast for warnings of icy or snowy weather. **DO NOT** drive in these conditions unless your journey is essential. If it is, take great care and allow more time for your journey. Take an emergency kit of de-icer and ice scraper, torch, warm clothing and boots, first aid kit, jump leads and a shovel, together with a warm drink and emergency food in case you get stuck or your vehicle breaks down.

229 Before you set off

- you **MUST** be able to see, so clear all snow and ice from all your windows
- you **MUST** ensure that lights are clean and number plates are clearly visible and legible
- make sure the mirrors are clear and the windows are demisted thoroughly
- remove all snow that might fall off into the path of other road users
- check your planned route is clear of delays and that no further snowfalls or severe weather are predicted.

Laws CUR reg 30, RVLR reg 23, VERA sect 43 & RV(DRM)R reg 11

Rule 229
Make sure your windscreen is completely clear

 When driving in icy or snowy weather

- drive with care, even if the roads have been treated

- keep well back from the road user in front as stopping distances can be ten times greater than on dry roads

- take care when overtaking vehicles spreading salt or other de-icer, particularly if you are riding a motorcycle or cycle

- watch out for snowploughs which may throw out snow on either side. Do not overtake them unless the lane you intend to use has been cleared

- be prepared for the road conditions to change over relatively short distances

- listen to travel bulletins and take note of variable message signs that may provide information about weather, road and traffic conditions ahead.

231 **Drive extremely carefully** when the roads are icy. Avoid sudden actions as these could cause loss of control. You should

- drive at a slow speed in as high a gear as possible; accelerate and brake very gently

- drive particularly slowly on bends where loss of control is more likely. Brake progressively on the straight before you reach a bend. Having slowed down, steer smoothly round the bend, avoiding sudden actions

- check your grip on the road surface when there is snow or ice by choosing a safe place to brake gently. If the steering feels unresponsive this may indicate ice and your vehicle losing its grip on the road. When travelling on ice, tyres make virtually no noise.

Windy weather

232 High-sided vehicles are most affected by windy weather, but strong gusts can also blow a car, cyclist, motorcyclist or horse rider off course. This can happen on open stretches of road exposed to strong crosswinds, or when passing bridges or gaps in hedges.

233 In very windy weather your vehicle may be affected by turbulence created by large vehicles. Motorcyclists are particularly affected, so keep well back from them when they are overtaking a high-sided vehicle.

Fog

234 **Before entering fog** check your mirrors then slow down.

If 'Fog' is shown on a sign but the road is clear, be prepared for a bank of fog or drifting patchy fog ahead. Even if it seems to be clearing, you can suddenly find yourself in thick fog.

235 **When driving in fog** you should

- use your lights as required (see Rule 226)
- keep a safe distance behind the vehicle in front. Rear lights can give a false sense of security
- be able to pull up well within the distance you can see clearly. This is particularly important on motorways and dual carriageways, as vehicles are travelling faster
- use your windscreen wipers and demisters
- beware of other drivers not using headlights

- not accelerate to get away from a vehicle which is too close behind you
- check your mirrors before you slow down. Then use your brakes so that your brake lights warn drivers behind you that you are slowing down
- stop in the correct position at a junction with limited visibility and listen for traffic. When you are sure it is safe to emerge, do so positively and do not hesitate in a position that puts you directly in the path of approaching vehicles.

236 You **MUST NOT** use front or rear fog lights unless visibility is seriously reduced (see Rule 226) as they dazzle other road users and can obscure your brake lights. You **MUST** switch them off when visibility improves.

Law RVLR regs 25 & 27

Hot weather

237 Keep your vehicle well ventilated to avoid drowsiness. Be aware that the road surface may become soft or if it rains after a dry spell it may become slippery. These conditions could affect your steering and braking. If you are dazzled by bright sunlight, slow down and if necessary, stop.

Waiting and parking

238 You **MUST NOT** wait or park on yellow lines during the times of operation shown on nearby time plates (or zone entry signs if in a Controlled Parking Zone) – see Traffic signs and Road markings. Double yellow lines indicate a prohibition of waiting at any time even if there are no upright signs. You **MUST NOT** wait or park, or stop to set down and pick up passengers, on school entrance markings (see Road markings) when upright signs indicate a prohibition of stopping.

Law RTRA sects 5 & 8

Parking and stopping

239 Use off-street parking areas, or bays marked out with white lines on the road as parking places, wherever possible. If you have to stop on the roadside

- do not park facing against the traffic flow

- stop as close as you can to the side

- do not stop too close to a vehicle displaying a Blue Badge: remember, the occupant may need more room to get in or out

- you **MUST** switch off the engine, headlights and fog lights

- you **MUST** apply the handbrake before leaving the vehicle

- you **MUST** ensure you do not hit anyone when you open your door. Check for cyclists or other traffic by looking all around and using your mirrors

Rule 239
Check
before
opening
your door

- where you are able to do so, you should open the door using your hand on the opposite side to the door you are opening; for example, use your left hand to open a door on your right-hand side. This will make you turn your head to look over your shoulder. You are then more likely to avoid causing injury to cyclists or motorcyclists passing you on the road, or to people on the pavement

- it is safer for your passengers (especially children) to get out of the vehicle on the side next to the kerb

- put all valuables out of sight and make sure your vehicle is secure

- lock your vehicle.

Before using a hand-held device to help you to park, you **MUST** make sure it is safe to do so. Then, you should move the vehicle into the parking space in the safest way, and by the shortest route possible.

When you use a hand-held device to help you to park, you **MUST** remain in control of the vehicle at all times. Do not use the hand-held device for anything else while you are using it to help you park, and **DO NOT** put anyone in danger. Use the hand-held device according to the manufacturer's instructions.

When using an electric vehicle charge point, you should park close to the charge point and avoid creating a trip hazard for pedestrians from trailing cables. Display a warning sign if you can. After using the charge point, you should return charging cables and connectors neatly to minimise the danger to pedestrians and avoid creating an obstacle for other road users.

Laws CUR regs 98, 105, 107 & 110, RVLR reg 27 & RTA 1988 sect 42

 You **MUST NOT** stop or park on

- the carriageway, an emergency area or a hard shoulder of a motorway except in an emergency (see Rules 270 and 271)

- a pedestrian crossing, including the area marked by the zig-zag lines (see Rule 191)

- a clearway (see Traffic signs)

- taxi bays as indicated by upright signs and markings

- an urban clearway within its hours of operation, except to pick up or set down passengers (see Traffic signs)

- a road marked with double white lines, even when a broken white line is on your side of the road, except to pick up or set down passengers, or to load or unload goods

- a tram or cycle lane during its period of operation

- a cycle track

- red lines, in the case of specially designated 'red routes', unless otherwise indicated by signs. Any vehicle may enter a bus lane to stop, load or unload where this is not prohibited (see Rule 141).

Laws MT(E&W)R regs 7 & 9 as amended by MT(E&W)(A)(E)R, MT(S)R regs 6 & 8, RTRA sects 5, 6 and 8, TSRGD schedule 7 parts 2, 3, 4, 6 and 7, schedule 9 part 6, schedule 14 parts 1 and 5

241
You **MUST NOT** park in parking spaces reserved for specific users, such as Blue Badge holders, residents or motorcycles, unless entitled to do so.

Laws CSDPA sect 21 & RTRA sects 5 & 8

242
You **MUST NOT** leave your vehicle or trailer in a dangerous position or where it causes any unnecessary obstruction of the road.

Laws RTA 1988 sect 22 & CUR reg 103

243
DO NOT stop or park

- near a school entrance
- anywhere you would prevent access for Emergency Services
- at or near a bus or tram stop or taxi rank
- on the approach to a level crossing/tramway crossing
- opposite or within 10 metres (32 feet) of a junction, except in an authorised parking space
- near the brow of a hill or hump bridge
- opposite a traffic island or (if this would cause an obstruction) another parked vehicle
- where you would force other traffic to enter a tram lane
- where the kerb has been lowered to help wheelchair users and powered mobility vehicles
- in front of an entrance to a property
- on a bend
- where you would obstruct cyclists' use of cycle facilities

except when forced to do so by stationary traffic.

244
You **MUST NOT** park partially or wholly on the pavement in London, and should not do so elsewhere unless signs permit

it. Parking on the pavement can obstruct and seriously inconvenience pedestrians, people in wheelchairs or with visual impairments and people with prams or pushchairs.

Law GL(GP)A sect 15

245 **Controlled Parking Zones.** The zone entry signs indicate the times when the waiting restrictions within the zone are in force. Parking may be allowed in some places at other times. Otherwise parking will be within separately signed and marked bays.

246 **Goods vehicles.** Vehicles with a maximum laden weight of over 7.5 tonnes (including any trailer) **MUST NOT** be parked on a verge, pavement or any land situated between carriageways, without police permission. The only exception is when parking is essential for loading and unloading, in which case the vehicle **MUST NOT** be left unattended.

Law RTA 1988 sect 19

247 **Loading and unloading.** Do not load or unload where there are yellow markings on the kerb and upright signs advise restrictions are in place (see Road markings). This may be permitted where parking is otherwise restricted. On red routes, specially marked and signed bays indicate where and when loading and unloading is permitted.

Law RTRA sects 5 & 8

Parking at night

248 You **MUST NOT** park on a road at night facing against the direction of the traffic flow unless in a recognised parking space.

Laws CUR reg 101 & RVLR reg 24

249 All vehicles **MUST** display parking lights when parked on a road or a lay-by on a road with a speed limit greater than 30 mph (48 km/h).

Law RVLR reg 24

250 Cars, goods vehicles not exceeding 2500 kg laden weight, invalid carriages, motorcycles and pedal cycles may be parked without lights on a road (or lay-by) with a speed limit of 30 mph (48 km/h) or less if they are

- at least 10 metres (32 feet) away from any junction, close to the kerb and facing in the direction of the traffic flow

- in a recognised parking place or lay-by.

Other vehicles and trailers, and all vehicles with projecting loads, **MUST NOT** be left on a road at night without lights.

Laws RVLR reg 24 & CUR reg 82(7)

Parking in fog

It is especially dangerous to park on the road in fog. If it is unavoidable, leave your parking lights or sidelights on.

Parking on hills

If you park on a hill you should

- park close to the kerb and apply the handbrake firmly

- select a forward gear and turn your steering wheel away from the kerb when facing uphill

- select reverse gear and turn your steering wheel towards the kerb when facing downhill

- use 'park' if your car has an automatic gearbox.

Rule 252
Turn your wheels away from the kerb when parking facing uphill. Turn them towards the kerb when parking facing downhill

Facing uphill

Facing downhill

Decriminalised Parking Enforcement (DPE)

DPE is becoming increasingly common as more authorities take on this role. The local traffic authority assumes responsibility for enforcing many parking contraventions in place of the police. Further details on DPE may be found at the following websites:

www.trafficpenaltytribunal.gov.uk (outside London)

www.londontribunals.gov.uk (inside London)

Motorways

A number of the rules for motorways also apply to other high-speed roads. Many other Rules apply to motorway driving, either wholly or in part: Rules 46, 57, 83–126, 130–134, 139, 144, 146–151, 160–161, 219, 221–222, 225, 226–237, 275–279, 280 and 281–290.

General

253

Prohibited vehicles. Motorways **MUST NOT** be used by pedestrians, holders of provisional motorcycle licences, riders of motorcycles under 50 cc (4 kW), cyclists, horse riders, certain slow-moving vehicles and those carrying oversized loads (except by special permission), agricultural vehicles, and powered wheelchairs/powered mobility scooters (see Rules 36 to 46 inclusive).

Provisional car licence holders **MUST NOT** drive on the motorway unless they are accompanied by a DVSA Approved Driving Instructor (ADI) and are driving a car displaying red L plates (or D plates in Wales) with dual controls.

Laws HA 1980 sects 16, 17 & sched 4, MT(E&W)R regs 3(d), 4 & 11 as amended by MT(E&W)(A)R 2004 & MT(E&W)(A)R 2018, R(S)A sects 7, 8 & sched 3, RTRA sect 17 & MT(S)R reg 10 as amended by MT(S)(A)R 2018

254

Traffic on motorways usually travels faster than on other roads, so you have less time to react. It is especially important to use your mirrors earlier and look much further ahead than you would on other roads.

Motorway signals

255 Signs and signals (see Light signals controlling traffic) are used to warn you of hazards ahead. For example, there may be an incident, fog, a spillage or road workers on the carriageway which you may not immediately be able to see.

256 A single sign or signal can display advice, restrictions and warnings for all lanes.

Lane specific signs and signals can display advice, restrictions and warnings that apply to individual lanes.

257 **Amber flashing lights.** These signals warn of a hazard ahead. You should

- reduce your speed

- be prepared for the hazard

- only increase your speed when you pass a signal that is not flashing, or a sign displaying a national speed limit or the word 'END', and you are sure it is safe to do so.

Rule 257
Signal warning of a hazard

258 **Red flashing light** signals and a red 'X' on a sign identify a closed lane in which people, stopped vehicles or other hazards are present. You

- **MUST** follow the instructions on signs in advance of a closed lane to move safely to an open lane

- **MUST NOT** drive in a closed lane. A sign will inform you when the lane is no longer closed by displaying a speed limit or the word 'END'.

Rule 258
Signals and signs indicating lane closures

Be aware that

- there can be several hazards in a closed lane

- emergency services and traffic authorities use closed lanes to reach incidents and help people in need

- where the left lane is closed at an exit slip road, this means that the exit cannot be used.

Where **red flashing light** signals and closure of all lanes are shown on a sign, the road is closed. You

- **MUST NOT** go beyond the sign in any lane or use the hard shoulder to avoid the road closure unless directed to do so by a police or traffic officer.

Lane and road closures indicated by red flashing lights are enforced by the police.

Laws RTA 1988 sects 35 & 36 as amended by TMA sect 6, TSRGD reg 3 and sched 15, MT(E&W)R reg 9 & MT(S)R reg 8.

Driving on the motorway

Joining the motorway. When you join the motorway you will normally approach it from a road on the left (a slip road) or from an adjoining motorway. You should

- give priority to traffic already on the motorway
- check the traffic on the motorway and match your speed to fit safely into the traffic flow in the left-hand lane
- not cross solid white lines that separate lanes or use the hard shoulder
- stay on the slip road if it continues as an extra lane on the motorway
- remain in the left-hand lane long enough to adjust to the speed of traffic before considering overtaking.

On the motorway

When you can see well ahead and the road conditions are good, you should

- drive at a steady cruising speed which you and your vehicle can handle safely and is within the speed limit (see Rule 124 and the Speed limits table)
- keep a safe distance from the vehicle in front and increase the gap on wet or icy roads, or in fog (see Rules 126 and 235).

You **MUST NOT** exceed

- a speed limit displayed within a red circle on a sign
- the maximum speed limit for the road and for your vehicle (see Rule 124).

Speed limits are enforced by the police (see Rule 124).

Law RTRA sects 17, 86, 89 & sched 6

The monotony of driving on motorways and other high-speed roads can make you feel sleepy. To minimise the risk, follow the advice in Rule 91 about ensuring you are fit to drive and taking breaks.

Service areas are located along motorways to allow you to take breaks and to obtain refreshments. Refreshment and rest facilities on the local road network may also be accessible from motorway exits.

Unless directed to do so by a police or traffic officer, you **MUST NOT**

- reverse along any part of a motorway, including slip roads, hard shoulders and emergency areas
- cross the central reservation
- drive against the traffic flow.

If you have missed your exit, or have taken the wrong route, carry on to the next exit.

Laws RTA 1988 sect 35 as amended by TMA sect 6, MT(E&W)R regs 6, 8 & 10, & MT(S)R regs 4, 5, 7 & 9

Lane discipline

Keep in the left lane unless overtaking.

- If you are overtaking, you should return to the left lane when it is safe to do so (see also Rules 267 and 268).
- Be aware of emergency services, traffic officers, recovery workers and other people or vehicles stopped on the hard shoulder or in an emergency area. If you are driving in the left lane, and it is safe to do so, you should move into the adjacent lane to create more space between your vehicle and the people and stopped vehicles.

265 The right-hand lane of a motorway with three or more lanes **MUST NOT** be used (except in prescribed circumstances) if you are driving

- any vehicle drawing a trailer

- a goods vehicle with a maximum laden weight exceeding 3.5 tonnes but not exceeding 7.5 tonnes, which is required to be fitted with a speed limiter

- a goods vehicle with a maximum laden weight exceeding 7.5 tonnes

- a passenger vehicle with a maximum laden weight exceeding 7.5 tonnes constructed or adapted to carry more than eight seated passengers in addition to the driver

- a passenger vehicle with a maximum laden weight not exceeding 7.5 tonnes which is constructed or adapted to carry more than eight seated passengers in addition to the driver, which is required to be fitted with a speed limiter.

Laws MT(E&W)R reg 12, MT(E&W)(A)R, MT(S)R reg 11 & MT(S)(A)R

266 **Approaching a junction.** Look well ahead for signals, signs and road markings. Direction signs may be placed over the road. If you need to, you should change lanes well ahead of a junction. At some junctions, a lane may lead directly off the road. Only get in that lane if you wish to go in the direction indicated by signs or road markings.

Overtaking

267 Do not overtake unless you are sure it is safe and legal to do so. Overtake only on the right. You should

- check your mirrors

- take time to judge the speeds correctly

- make sure that the lane you will be joining is sufficiently clear ahead and behind

- take a quick sideways glance into the blind spot area to verify the position of a vehicle that may have disappeared from your view in the mirror

- remember that traffic may be coming up behind you very quickly. Check all your mirrors carefully. Look out for motor cyclists. When it is safe to do so, signal in plenty of time, then move out
- ensure you do not cut in on the vehicle you have overtaken
- be especially careful at night and in poor visibility when it is harder to judge speed and distance.

268 Do not overtake on the left or move to a lane on your left to overtake. In congested conditions, where adjacent lanes of traffic are moving at similar speeds, traffic in left-hand lanes may sometimes be moving faster than traffic to the right. In these conditions you may keep up with the traffic in your lane even if this means passing traffic in the lane to your right. Do not weave in and out of lanes to overtake.

Hard shoulder

269 **Hard shoulder** (where present). You **MUST NOT** use a hard shoulder except in an emergency or if directed to do so by the police, traffic officers or a traffic sign.

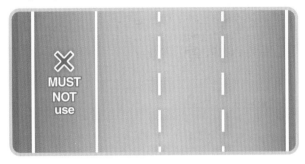

Hard shoulder (where used as an extra lane). The hard shoulder is used as an extra lane on some motorways during periods of congestion. A red 'X' or blank sign above the hard shoulder means that you **MUST NOT** use the hard shoulder except in an emergency.

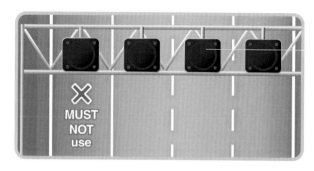

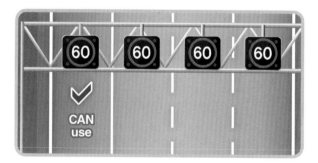

You can only use the hard shoulder as an extra lane when a speed limit is shown above the hard shoulder.

Where the hard shoulder is being used as an extra lane, emergency areas are provided for use in an emergency (see Rule 270).

Laws MT(E&W)R regs 5 & 9, MT(S)R regs 4 & 8, & RTA 1988 sects 35 & 36 as amended by TMA sect 6

Stopping

Emergency areas are located along motorways with no hard shoulder or where the hard shoulder can be used as an extra lane (see Rule 269) and **MUST** only be used in an emergency.

They are marked by blue signs with an orange SOS telephone symbol and may have orange surfacing.

Rule 270
Emergency area and sign indicating distance to next emergency area

Follow the requirements and advice in

* Rule 277 if your vehicle develops a problem on the motorway

* Rule 278 to rejoin the carriageway from an emergency area.

Laws MT(E&W)R reg 9 as amended by MT(E&W)(A)(E)R, & MT(S)R reg 8

You **MUST NOT** stop on any carriageway, emergency area, hard shoulder, slip road, central reservation or verge except in an emergency, or when told to do so by the police, traffic officers, an emergency sign or by red flashing light signals.

Do not stop on any part of a motorway to make or receive mobile telephone calls, except in an emergency.

Laws MT(E&W)R regs 7, 9, 10 & 16 as amended by MT(E&W)(A)(E)R, MT(S)R regs 6(1), 8, 9 & 14, PRA sect 41 & sched 5(8), RTA 1988 sects 35, 36 & 163 as amended by TMA sect 6, & CUR reg 110 as amended by CUR(A)(No4)R

You **MUST NOT** pick up or set down anyone, or walk on a motorway, except in an emergency.

Laws RTRA sect 17 & MT(E&W)R reg 15

Leaving the motorway

273 Unless signs indicate that a lane leads directly off the motorway, you will normally leave the motorway by a slip road on your left. You should

- watch for the signs letting you know you are getting near your exit
- move into the left-hand lane well before reaching your exit
- signal left in good time and reduce your speed on the slip road as necessary.

274 On leaving the motorway or using a link road between motorways, your speed may be higher than you realise – 50 mph may feel like 30 mph. Check your speedometer and adjust your speed accordingly. Some slip roads and link roads have sharp bends, so you will need to slow down.

Breakdowns and incidents

Place of relative safety

275 If you need to stop your vehicle in the event of a breakdown or incident, try to stop in a place of relative safety. A place of relative safety is where you, your passengers and your vehicle are less likely to be at risk from moving traffic.

The safest place to stop is a location which is designed for parking. On motorways and other high-speed roads, the safest place to stop is a service area. Other places of relative safety include

- lay-bys
- emergency areas (see Rule 270)
- hard shoulders (see Rule 269).

Be aware that hard shoulders provide less protection than other places of relative safety because they are so close to high-speed traffic.

You and your passengers should, where possible, keep well away from your vehicle and moving traffic. Otherwise moving traffic could collide with your vehicle, forcing it into you and your passengers.

Breakdowns

If your vehicle breaks down, think first of all other road users and

- get your vehicle off the road if possible
- warn other traffic by using your hazard warning lights if your vehicle is causing an obstruction
- help other road users see you by wearing light-coloured or fluorescent clothing in daylight and reflective clothing at night or in poor visibility
- put a warning triangle on the road at least 45 metres (147 feet) behind your broken-down vehicle on the same side of the road, or use other permitted warning devices if you have them. Always take great care when placing or retrieving them, but never use them on motorways
- if possible, keep your sidelights on if it is dark or visibility is poor
- do not stand (or let anybody else stand) between your vehicle and oncoming traffic
- at night or in poor visibility do not stand where you will prevent other road users seeing your lights.

Additional rules for the motorway and other high-speed roads

If your vehicle develops a problem, leave the carriageway at the next exit or pull into a service area if possible (see Rule 275 for places of relative safety). If you cannot, you should

Go left

- move into the left lane
- pull into an emergency area or onto a hard shoulder if you can
- stop as far to the left as possible, leaving space to exit your vehicle and with your wheels turned to the left
- if you can, stop just beyond an emergency telephone

- switch your hazard warning lights on

- if it's dark or visibility is poor, use sidelights.

Get safe

- exit your vehicle by the side furthest from traffic, if it is safe and possible to do so, and ensure passengers do the same

If you can't
- **get your vehicle to the left lane or a place of relative safety (see Rule 275), and**
- **exit your vehicle safely to get well away from it and moving traffic,**

you should
- **stay in your vehicle**
- **keep your seat belts and hazard warning lights on**
- **call 999 immediately and ask for the police. Alternatively, press your SOS button if your vehicle has one and ask for the police.**

- put on high-visibility clothing if you have it and it is within easy reach

- get behind a safety barrier where there is one, but be aware of any unseen hazards such as sudden drops, uneven ground or debris

- **DO NOT** stand in a place where your vehicle could be forced into you if moving traffic collides with it

- **DO NOT** return to your vehicle even if it's raining, cold or dark

- remain alert and aware of vehicles or debris coming towards you

- keep passengers away from the carriageway and children under control

- **DO NOT** attempt repairs on your vehicle

- **DO NOT** place a warning triangle on the carriageway

- animals **MUST** be kept in the vehicle or, in an emergency, under control on the verge.

Rule 277
Keep well away from your vehicle and moving traffic

Get help

- use the free emergency telephone to obtain advice and assistance

- contact a breakdown recovery service

- always face the traffic when you speak to remain aware of vehicles or debris coming towards you

- inform them if you are a vulnerable motorist such as disabled, older or travelling alone

- wait well away from your vehicle and moving traffic, behind the safety barrier where there is one

- if you are unable to exit your vehicle or if you have not stopped near a free emergency telephone, call 999 immediately and ask for the police. Alternatively, press your SOS button if your vehicle has one and ask for the police.

Communicating your location. How to identify your location to the emergency services.

eCall

Press the SOS button if your vehicle has one.

App

Use a mobile telephone mapping application.

Marker post or driver location sign

Quote the numbers and letters on marker posts or driver location signs which are located along the edge of the road.

Laws MT(E&W)R reg 14 & MT(S)R reg 12

278 To rejoin the carriageway after a breakdown from

- a hard shoulder, build up speed, indicate and watch for a safe gap in the traffic. Be aware that vehicles, obstructions or debris may be present on the hard shoulder

- an emergency area, you **MUST** use the emergency telephone provided and follow the operator's advice for exiting the emergency area. A lane may need to be closed so that you can rejoin the carriageway safely.

Rule 278
Emergency
area
information
sign

Law RTA 1988 sect 36

279 **Disabled drivers.** If you have a disability that prevents you from following the above advice in Rules 277 and 278, you should

- switch on your hazard warning lights

- stay in your vehicle and keep your seat belt on

- call 999 immediately and ask for the police. Alternatively, press your SOS button if your vehicle has one and ask for the police.

If you are deaf, hard of hearing or speech impaired, it is recommended that you register for the 999 text service (emergencySMS.net) before making a journey.

Obstructions

280 If anything falls from a vehicle on to a motorway or other high-speed road, **DO NOT** remove the obstruction yourself. Stop in a place of relative safety (see Rule 275) and call the emergency services on 999.

On other roads, you should only remove obstructions if it is safe to do so.

Incidents

 Warning signs or flashing lights. If you see emergency or incident support vehicles displaying flashing lights in the distance, be aware there may be an incident ahead (see Rule 219). You should slow down and be prepared to move safely into another lane or stop.

The emergency services, traffic officers and recovery workers may be required to work in the carriageway; for example, dealing with debris, collisions or conducting rolling roadblocks. You **MUST** follow any directions given by police or traffic officers as to whether you can safely pass the incident or obstruction.

Laws RTA 1988 sects 35 & 163 as amended by TMA sect 6

 When passing the scene of an incident, remain alert for hazards (such as debris or slow-moving vehicles) and do not slow down unnecessarily (for example, if an incident is on the other side of a dual carriageway). You should focus on the road ahead when passing an incident because a lack of attention may cause a further incident, collision or congestion (see also Rule 283, below).

 If you are involved in an incident or collision or stop to give assistance

- if possible, stop in a place of relative safety (see Rule 275)

- use your hazard warning lights to warn other traffic

- put on high-visibility clothing if you have it

- ask drivers to switch off their engines

- ask drivers and passengers to stop smoking

- contact the emergency services on 999 and provide full details of the incident location and any casualties. Use an emergency telephone, a mobile telephone, or press the SOS button if your vehicle has one (see Rule 277 on how to identify your location on a motorway or other high-speed road)

- move uninjured people away from the vehicles to a place of relative safety (see Rule 275)

- **DO NOT** move injured people from their vehicles unless they are in immediate danger

- **DO NOT** remove a motorcyclist's helmet unless it is essential and you are trained to do so

- be prepared to give first aid (see Annex 7 and Useful websites)

- stay at the scene until the emergency services arrive

- be prepared to exchange details (see Rule 286).

If you are involved in any other medical emergency, you should contact the emergency services in the same way.

Incidents involving dangerous goods

 Vehicles carrying dangerous goods in packages will be marked with plain orange reflective plates. Road tankers and vehicles carrying tank containers of dangerous goods will have hazard warning plates (see Vehicle markings).

 If an incident involves a vehicle containing dangerous goods, follow the advice in Rule 283 and, in particular

- switch off engines and **DO NOT SMOKE**

- keep well away from the vehicle and do not be tempted to try to rescue casualties as you yourself could become one

- call the emergency services and give as much information as possible about the labels and markings on the vehicle. **DO NOT** use a mobile phone close to a vehicle carrying flammable loads.

Documentation

If you are involved in a collision which causes damage or injury to any other person, vehicle, animal or property, you **MUST**

- stop. If possible, stop in a place of relative safety (see Rule 275)

- give your own and the vehicle owner's name and address, and the registration number of the vehicle, to anyone having reasonable grounds for requiring them

- if you do not give your name and address at the time of the collision, report it to the police as soon as reasonably practicable, and in any case within 24 hours.

Law RTA 1988 sect 170

287 If another person is injured and you do not produce your insurance certificate at the time of the crash to a police officer or to anyone having reasonable grounds to request it, you **MUST**

- report it to the police as soon as possible and in any case within 24 hours
- produce your insurance certificate for the police within seven days.

Law RTA 1988 sect 170

Road works

288 When the 'Road Works Ahead' sign is displayed, take extra care and look for additional signs providing more specific instructions. Observe all signs – they are there for your safety and the safety of road workers.

- You **MUST NOT** exceed any temporary maximum speed limit.
- Keep a safe distance from the vehicle in front (see Rule 126).
- Use your mirrors and get into the correct lane for your vehicle in good time and as signs direct.
- Do not switch lanes to overtake queuing traffic.
- Take extra care near cyclists and motorcyclists as they are vulnerable to skidding on grit, mud or other debris at road works.
- Where lanes are restricted due to road works, merge in turn (see Rule 134).
- Do not drive through an area marked off by traffic cones.
- Watch out for vehicles entering or leaving the works area. Where vehicles are travelling in the road and are displaying amber warning lights, leave extra space and expect them to slow or turn into a works area.
- Concentrate on the road ahead, not the road works.

- Bear in mind that the road ahead may be obstructed by the works or by slow-moving or stationary traffic.

Law RTRA sect 16

Additional rules for high-speed roads

Take special care on motorways and other high-speed dual carriageways.

- Lanes may be closed to traffic and a lower speed limit may apply.

- Works vehicles may be used to close lanes or carriageways for repairs. Where large 'Keep Left' or 'Keep Right' signs are displayed on the back, you **MUST** move over and pass the works vehicle on the side indicated and not return to the closed lane until you can see it is safe to do so.

- Where a vehicle displays the sign 'CONVOY VEHICLE NO OVERTAKING', you **MUST NOT** pass the vehicle. A flashing light arrow or red 'X' may also be used to make the works vehicle more visible from a distance and give earlier warning to drivers.

Laws RTA 1988 sect 36, TSRGD reg 3 and sched 13

Road works may contain features that require extra care.

- **Narrow lanes.** Lanes may be narrower than normal and will be marked by studs or temporary road markings. Keep a safe distance (see Rule 126) from the vehicle in front and make sure you can clearly see the edges of the lane ahead.

- **Contraflow systems.** These mean that you may be travelling in a narrower lane than normal and with no permanent barrier between you and oncoming traffic. At the start and finish of contraflows, you should slow down and increase the distance to the vehicle in front because changes in the camber of the road may affect vehicle stability.

- **Breakdown advice.** If your vehicle breaks down in road works, follow Rules 275, 277 and 278 but be aware that areas marked off by cones contain significant hazards. Where available, you should move your vehicle into a signed road works refuge location. Signs indicate where dedicated recovery services are provided.

Level crossings

291 A level crossing is where a road crosses a railway or tramway line. Approach and cross it with care. Never drive onto a crossing until the road is clear on the other side and do not get too close to the car in front. Never stop or park on, or near, a crossing.

292 **Overhead electric lines.** It is dangerous to touch overhead electric lines. You **MUST** obey the safe height warning road signs and you should not continue forward onto the railway if your vehicle touches any height barrier or bells. The clearance available is usually 5 metres (16 feet 6 inches) but may be lower.

Laws RTA 1988 sect 36 & TSRGD schedule 2 part 7

293 **Controlled crossings.** Most crossings have traffic light signals with a steady amber light, twin flashing red stop lights (see Light signals controlling traffic and Traffic signs) and an audible alarm for pedestrians. They may have full, half or no barriers.

- You **MUST** always obey the flashing red stop lights.

- You **MUST** stop behind the white line across the road.

- Keep going if you have already crossed the white line when the amber light comes on.

- Do not reverse onto or over a controlled crossing.

- You **MUST** wait if a train goes by and the red lights continue to flash. This means another train will be passing soon.

- Only cross when the lights go off and barriers open.

Rule 293
Stop when the traffic lights show

- Never zig-zag around half-barriers, they lower automatically because a train is approaching.

- At crossings where there are no barriers, a train is approaching when the lights show.

Laws RTA 1988 sect 36 & TSRGD schedule 14 parts 1 and 4

294 **Railway telephones.** If you are driving a large or slow-moving vehicle, a long, low vehicle with a risk of grounding, or herding animals, a train could arrive before you are clear of the crossing. You **MUST** obey any sign instructing you to use the railway telephone to obtain permission to cross. You **MUST** also telephone when clear of the crossing if requested to do so.

Laws RTA 1988 sect 36 & TSRGD schedule 9 parts 7 and 8

295 **Crossings without traffic lights.** Vehicles should stop and wait at the barrier or gate when it begins to close and not cross until the barrier or gate opens.

296 **User-operated gates or barriers.** Some crossings have 'Stop' signs and small red and green lights. You **MUST NOT** cross when the red light is showing, only cross if the green light is on. If crossing with a vehicle, you should

- open the gates or barriers on both sides of the crossing

- check that the green light is still on and cross quickly

- close the gates or barriers when you are clear of the crossing.

Laws TWA 1992 sect 55 & PC(SB)R 1996

297 If there are no lights, follow the procedure in Rule 296. Stop, look both ways and listen before you cross. If there is a railway telephone, always use it to contact the signal operator to make sure it is safe to cross. Inform the signal operator again when you are clear of the crossing.

298 **Open crossings.** These have no gates, barriers, attendant or traffic lights but will have a 'Give Way' sign. You should look both ways, listen and make sure there is no train coming before you cross.

299 **Incidents and breakdowns.** If your vehicle breaks down, or if you have an incident on a crossing, you should

- get everyone out of the vehicle and clear of the crossing immediately

- use a railway telephone if available to tell the signal operator. Follow the instructions you are given

- move the vehicle clear of the crossing if there is time before a train arrives. If the alarm sounds, or the amber light comes on, leave the vehicle and get clear of the crossing immediately.

Tramways

300 You **MUST NOT** enter a road, lane or other route reserved for trams. Take extra care where trams run along the road. You should avoid driving directly on top of the rails and should take care where trams leave the main carriageway to enter the reserved route, to ensure you do not follow them. The width taken up by trams is often shown by tram lanes marked by white lines, yellow dots or by a different type of road surface. Diamond-shaped signs and white light signals give instructions to tram drivers only.

Law RTRA sects 5 & 8

301 Take extra care where the track crosses from one side of the road to the other and where the road narrows and the tracks come close to the kerb. Tram drivers usually have their own traffic signals and may be permitted to move when you are not. Always give way to trams. Do not try to race or overtake them or pass them on the inside, unless they are at tram stops or stopped by tram signals and there is a designated tram lane for you to pass.

302 You **MUST NOT** park your vehicle where it would get in the way of trams or where it would force other drivers to do so. Do not stop on any part of a tram track, except in a designated bay where this has been provided alongside and clear of the track. When doing so, ensure that all parts of your vehicle are outside the delineated tram path. Remember that a tram cannot steer round an obstruction.
Law RTRA sects 5 & 8

303 **Tram stops.** Where the tram stops at a platform, either in the middle or at the side of the road, you **MUST** follow the route shown by the road signs and markings. At stops without platforms you **MUST NOT** drive between a tram and the left-hand kerb when a tram has stopped to pick up passengers. If there is no alternative route signed, do not overtake the tram – wait until it moves off.
Law RTRA sects 5 & 8

304 Look out for pedestrians, especially children, running to catch a tram approaching a stop.

305 Always give priority to trams, especially when they signal to pull away from stops, unless it would be unsafe to do so. Remember that they may be carrying large numbers of standing passengers who could be injured if the tram had to make an emergency stop. Look out for people getting off a bus or tram and crossing the road.

306 All road users, but particularly cyclists and motorcyclists, should take extra care when driving or riding close to or crossing the tracks, especially if the rails are wet. You should take particular care when crossing the rails at shallow angles, on bends and at junctions. It is safest to cross the tracks directly at right angles. Other road users should be aware that cyclists and motorcyclists may need more space to cross the tracks safely.

307

Overhead electric lines. Tramway overhead wires are normally 5.8 metres above any carriageway, but can be lower. You should ensure that you have sufficient clearance between the wire and your vehicle (including any load you are carrying) before driving under an overhead wire. Drivers of vehicles with extending cranes, booms, tipping apparatus or other types of variable height equipment should ensure that the equipment is fully lowered. Where overhead wires are set lower than 5.8 metres, these will be indicated by height clearance markings – similar to 'low bridge' signs. The height clearances on these plates should be carefully noted and observed. If you are in any doubt as to whether your vehicle will pass safely under the wires, you should always contact the local police or the tramway operator. Never take a chance as this can be extremely hazardous.

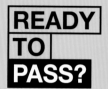

READY TO PASS?

Supported by
AA Driving School

Get ready for your driving test

Get ready to pass your driving test by checking our advice and tips for learner drivers.

www.gov.uk/ready-to-pass

Driver & Vehicle
Standards
Agency

Keep your phone in here if you want to keep your licence.

It's 6 points if you hold and use your phone while driving. If you've passed your test in the last 2 years, you'll lose your licence.

THINK!
PUT YOUR PHONE
AWAY

Light signals controlling traffic

Traffic light signals

RED means 'Stop'. Wait behind the stop line on the carriageway

RED AND AMBER also means 'Stop'. Do not pass through or start until GREEN shows

GREEN means you may go on if the way is clear. Take special care if you intend to turn left or right and give way to pedestrians who are crossing

AMBER means 'Stop' at the stop line. You may go on only if the AMBER appears after you have crossed the stop line or are so close to it that to pull up might cause an accident

A GREEN ARROW may be provided in addition to the full green signal if movement in a certain direction is allowed before or after the full green phase. If the way is clear you may go but only in the direction shown by the arrow. You may do this whatever other lights may be showing. White light signals may be provided for trams

Flashing red lights

Alternately flashing red lights mean YOU MUST STOP

At level crossings, lifting bridges, airfields, fire stations, etc.

Motorway signals

These signals are also used on other high-speed roads.

You **MUST NOT** proceed further in this lane

Change lane

Reduced visibility ahead

Lane ahead closed

Temporary maximum speed advised and information message

You **MUST NOT** enter or proceed in the left lane, temporary mandatory maximum speed limit and information message

Temporary maximum speed advised

End of restriction

Lane control signals

Green arrow – lane available to traffic facing the sign
Red crosses – lane closed to traffic facing the sign
White diagonal arrow – change lanes in direction shown

Signals to other road users

Direction indicator signals

I intend to move out to the right or turn right

I intend to move in to the left or turn left or stop on the left

Brake light signals

Reversing light signals

Hazard lights

I am applying the brakes

I intend to reverse

I am temporarily obstructing traffic or warning of a hazard or obstruction ahead (see Rule 116)

These signals should not be used except for the purposes described.

Arm signals

For use when direction indicator signals are not used, or when necessary to reinforce direction indicator signals and stop lights. **Also for use by pedal cyclists and those in charge of horses.**

I intend to move in to the left or turn left

I intend to move out to the right or turn right

I intend to slow down or stop

Signals by authorised persons

Police officers

Stop

Traffic approaching from the front

Traffic approaching from both front and behind

Traffic approaching from behind

To beckon traffic on

From the side

From the front

From behind*

Arm signals to persons controlling traffic

I want to go straight on

I want to turn left; use either hand

I want to turn right

* In Wales, bilingual signs appear on emergency services vehicles and clothing

Driver and Vehicle Standards Agency officers and traffic officers

Traffic officer

DVSA officer

These officers now have new powers to stop/direct vehicles and will be using hand signals and light signals similar to those used by police. You **MUST** obey any signals given (see Rules 107 and 108).

School crossing patrols

Not ready to cross pedestrians

Barrier to stop pedestrians crossing

Ready to cross pedestrians, vehicles must be prepared to stop

All vehicles must stop

Traffic signs

Signs giving orders

Signs with red circles are mostly prohibitive.
Plates below signs qualify their message.

Entry to
20 mph zone

End of
20 mph
zone

Maximum
speed

National speed
limit applies

School crossing
patrol

Stop and
give way

Give way to
traffic on
major road

Manually operated temporary
STOP and GO signs

No entry for
vehicular traffic

No vehicles
except bicycles
being pushed

No cycling

No motor
vehicles

No buses
(over 8
passenger
seats)

No
overtaking

No
towed
caravans

No vehicles
carrying
explosives

No vehicle or
combination of vehicles
over length shown

No vehicles
over
height shown

No vehicles
over
width shown

Give priority to
vehicles from
opposite
direction

No right turn

No left turn

No
U-turns

No goods vehicles
over maximum
gross weight
shown (in tonnes)
except for loading
and unloading

Note: Although *The Highway Code* shows many of the signs commonly in use, a comprehensive
explanation of our signing system is given in the Department's booklet *Know Your Traffic Signs*,
which is on sale at booksellers. The booklet also illustrates and explains the vast majority of signs
the road user is likely to encounter. The signs illustrated in *The Highway Code* are not all drawn to
the same scale. In Wales, bilingual versions of some signs are used including Welsh and English
versions of place names. Some older designs of signs may still be seen on the roads.

No vehicles
over maximum
gross weight
shown
(in tonnes)

Parking restricted
to permit holders

No stopping during
period indicated
except for buses

No stopping during
times shown
except for as long
as necessary to set
down or pick up
passengers

No waiting

No stopping
(Clearway)

Signs with blue circles but no red border mostly give positive instruction.

Ahead only

Turn left ahead
(right if symbol
reversed)

Turn left
(right if symbol
reversed)

Keep left
(right if symbol
reversed)

Vehicles
may pass
either side to
reach same
destination

Mini-roundabout
(roundabout
circulation –
give way to
vehicles from the
immediate right)

Route to be
used by pedal
cycles only

Segregated
pedal cycle
and pedestrian
route

Minimum speed

End of minimum
speed

Buses and
cycles
only

Trams only

Pedestrian
crossing
point over
tramway

One-way traffic
(note: compare
circular 'Ahead
only' sign)

With-flow bus and
cycle lane

Contra-flow bus lane

With-flow pedal cycle lane

Warning signs

Mostly triangular

Distance to 'STOP' line ahead

Dual carriageway ends

Road narrows on right (left if symbol reversed)

Road narrows on both sides

Distance to 'Give Way' line ahead

Crossroads

Junction on bend ahead

T-junction with priority over vehicles from the right

Staggered junction

Traffic merging from left ahead

The priority through route is indicated by the broader line.

Double bend first to left (symbol may be reversed)

Bend to right (or left if symbol reversed)

Roundabout

Uneven road

Plate below some signs

Two-way traffic crosses one-way road

Two-way traffic straight ahead

Opening or swing bridge ahead

Low-flying aircraft or sudden aircraft noise

Falling or fallen rocks

Traffic signals not in use

Traffic signals

Slippery road

Steep hill downwards

Steep hill upwards

Gradients may be shown as a ratio i.e. 20% = 1:5

Tunnel ahead

Trams crossing ahead

Level crossing with barrier or gate ahead

Level crossing without barrier or gate ahead

Level crossing without barrier

Warning signs – continued

School crossing patrol ahead (some signs have amber lights which flash when crossings are in use)

Frail (or blind or disabled if shown) pedestrians likely to cross road ahead

Pedestrians in road ahead

Zebra crossing

Overhead electric cable; plate indicates maximum height of vehicles which can pass safely

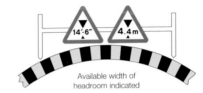

Available width of headroom indicated

Sharp deviation of route to left (or right if chevrons reversed)

Light signals ahead at level crossing, airfield or bridge

Miniature warning lights at level crossings

Cattle

Wild animals

Wild horses or ponies

Accompanied horses or ponies

Cycle route ahead

Risk of ice

Traffic queues likely ahead

Distance over which road humps extend

Other danger; plate indicates nature of danger

Soft verges

Side winds

Hump bridge

Worded warning sign

Quayside or river bank

Risk of grounding

Direction signs

Mostly rectangular

Signs on motorways – blue backgrounds

At a junction leading directly into a motorway (junction number may be shown on a black background)

On approaches to junctions (junction number on black background)

Route confirmatory sign after junction

Downward pointing arrows mean 'Get in lane'
The left-hand lane leads to a different destination from the other lanes.

The panel with the inclined arrow indicates the destinations which can be reached by leaving the motorway at the next junction

Signs on primary routes – green backgrounds

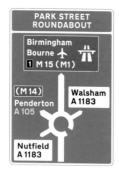

On approaches to junctions

At the junction

Route confirmatory sign after junction

On approaches to junctions

On approach to a junction in Wales (bilingual)

Blue panels indicate that the motorway starts at the junction ahead.
Motorways shown in brackets can also be reached along the route indicated.
White panels indicate local or non-primary routes leading from the junction ahead.
Brown panels show the route to tourist attractions.
The name of the junction may be shown at the top of the sign.
The aircraft symbol indicates the route to an airport.
A symbol may be included to warn of a hazard or restriction along that route.

Green background signs – continued

On approaches to junctions

Primary route forming
part of a ring road

Signs on non-primary and local routes – black borders

On approaches to junctions

At the junction

Direction to toilets
with access for the
disabled

Green panels indicate that the primary route starts at the junction ahead.
Route numbers on a blue background show the direction to a motorway.
Route numbers on a green background show the direction to a primary route.

Other direction signs

Picnic site

Ancient monument in the care
of English Heritage

Direction to a car park

Tourist attraction

Direction to camping
and caravan site

Advisory route for lorries

Route for pedal
cycles forming part
of a network

Recommended route for
pedal cycles to place shown

Route for pedestrians

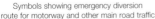

Symbols showing emergency diversion
route for motorway and other main road traffic

Diversion route

Information signs

All rectangular

Entrance to controlled parking zone

Entrance to congestion charging zone

End of controlled parking zone

Advance warning of restriction or prohibition ahead

Parking place for solo motorcycles

With-flow bus lane ahead which pedal cycles and taxis may also use

Lane designated for use by high occupancy vehicles (HOV) – see Rule 142

Vehicles permitted to use an HOV lane ahead

End of motorway

Start of motorway and point from which motorway regulations apply

Appropriate traffic lanes at junction ahead

Traffic on the main carriageway coming from right has priority over joining traffic

Additional traffic joining from left ahead. Traffic on main carriageway has priority over joining traffic from right hand lane of slip road

Traffic in right hand lane of slip road joining the main carriageway has priority over left hand lane

Variable speed limit with camera enforcement sign

'Countdown' markers at exit from motorway (each bar represents 100 yards to the exit). Green-backed markers may be used on primary routes and white-backed markers with black bars on other routes. At approaches to concealed level crossings white-backed markers with red bars may be used. Although these will be erected at equal distances the bars do not represent 100 yard intervals.

Motorway service area sign showing the operator's name

Information signs – continued

Traffic has priority over oncoming vehicles

Hospital ahead with Accident and Emergency facilities

Tourist information point

No through road for vehicles

Recommended route for pedal cycles

Home Zone Entry

Area in which cameras are used to enforce traffic regulations

Bus lane on road at junction ahead

Road works signs

Road works

Loose chippings

Temporary hazard at road works

Temporary lane closure (the number and position of arrows and red bars may be varied according to lanes open and closed)

Slow-moving or stationary works vehicle blocking a traffic lane. Pass in the direction shown by the arrow.

Mandatory speed limit ahead

Road works 1 mile ahead

End of road works and any temporary restrictions including speed limits

Signs used on the back of slow-moving or stationary vehicles warning of a lane closed ahead by a works vehicle. There are no cones on the road.

Lane restrictions at road works ahead

One lane crossover at contraflow road works

Road markings

Across the carriageway

Stop line at signals or police control

Stop line at 'Stop' sign

Stop line for pedestrians at a level crossing

Give way to traffic on major road (can also be used at mini roundabouts)

Give way to traffic from the right at a roundabout

Give way to traffic from the right at a mini-roundabout

Along the carriageway

Edge line

Centre line
See Rule 127

Hazard warning line
See Rule 127

Double white lines
See Rules 128 and 129

See Rule 130

Lane line
See Rule 131

Along the edge of the carriageway

Waiting restrictions

Waiting restrictions indicated by yellow lines apply to the carriageway, pavement and verge. You may stop to load or unload (unless there are also loading restrictions as described below) or while passengers board or alight. Double yellow lines mean no waiting at any time, unless there are signs that specifically indicate seasonal restrictions. The times at which the restrictions apply for other road markings are shown on nearby plates or on entry signs to controlled parking zones. If no days are shown on the signs, the restrictions are in force every day including Sundays and Bank Holidays. White bay markings and upright signs (see below) indicate where parking is allowed.

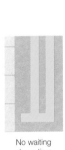

No waiting
at any time

No waiting
during times
shown on sign

Waiting is limited to the
duration specified during the
days and times shown

Red Route stopping controls

Red lines are used on some roads instead of yellow lines. In London the double and single red lines used on Red Routes indicate that stopping to park, load/unload or to board and alight from a vehicle (except for a licensed taxi or if you hold a Blue Badge) is prohibited. The red lines apply to the carriageway, pavement and verge. The times that the red line prohibitions apply are shown on nearby signs, but the double red line ALWAYS means no stopping at any time. On Red Routes you may stop to park, load/unload in specially marked boxes and adjacent signs specify the times and purposes and duration allowed. A box MARKED IN RED indicates that it may only be available for the purpose specified for part of the day (eg between busy peak periods). A box MARKED IN WHITE means that it is available throughout the day.

RED AND SINGLE YELLOW LINES CAN ONLY GIVE A GUIDE TO THE RESTRICTIONS AND CONTROLS IN FORCE AND SIGNS, NEARBY OR AT A ZONE ENTRY, MUST BE CONSULTED.

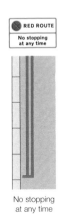

No stopping
at any time

No stopping
during times
shown on sign

Parking is limited to the
duration specified during
the days and times shown

Only loading may take
place at the times shown
for up to a maximum
duration of 20 mins

On the kerb or at the edge of the carriageway

Loading restrictions on roads other than Red Routes

Yellow marks on the kerb or at the edge of the carriageway indicate that loading or unloading is prohibited at the times shown on the nearby black and white plates. You may stop while passengers board or alight. If no days are indicated on the signs the restrictions are in force every day including Sundays and Bank Holidays.

ALWAYS CHECK THE TIMES SHOWN ON THE PLATES.

Lengths of road reserved for vehicles loading and unloading are indicated by a white 'bay' marking with the words 'Loading Only' and a sign with the white on blue 'trolley' symbol. This sign also shows whether loading and unloading is restricted to goods vehicles and the times at which the bay can be used. If no times or days are shown it may be used at any time. Vehicles may not park here if they are not loading or unloading.

No loading or unloading
at any time

No loading or unloading
at the times shown

Loading bay

Other road markings

Keep entrance clear of stationary vehicles, even if picking up or setting down children

Warning of 'Give Way'
just ahead

Parking space reserved
for vehicles named

See Rule 243

See Rule 141

Box junction – see Rule 174

Do not block that part of
the carriageway indicated

Indication of traffic lanes

136

Vehicle markings

Large goods vehicle rear markings

Motor vehicles over 7500 kilograms maximum gross weight and trailers over 3500 kilograms maximum gross weight

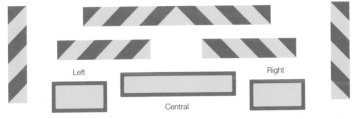

Left

Right

Central

The vertical markings are also required to be fitted to builders' skips placed in the road, commercial vehicles or combinations longer than 13 metres (optional on combinations between 11 and 13 metres)

Hazard warning plates

Certain tank vehicles carrying dangerous goods must display hazard information panels

The panel illustrated is for flammable liquid. Diamond symbols indicating other risks include:

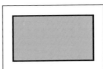

The above panel will be displayed by vehicles carrying certain dangerous goods in packages

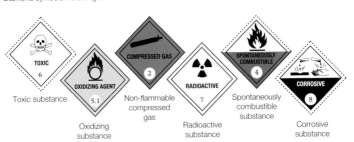

Toxic substance

Oxidizing substance

Non-flammable compressed gas

Radioactive substance

Spontaneously combustible substance

Corrosive substance

Projection markers

Side marker

End marker

Both required when load or equipment (eg crane jib) overhangs front or rear by more than two metres

Other

School bus (displayed in front or rear window of bus or coach)

Annexes

1. You and your bicycle

Make sure that you feel confident of your ability to ride safely on the road. Be sure that

- you have the right size and type of cycle for your comfort and safety
- the lights and reflectors are kept clean and in good working order
- the tyres are in good condition and inflated to the pressure shown on the tyre
- the wheels spin freely
- the gears are working correctly
- the chain is properly adjusted and oiled
- the saddle and handlebars are adjusted to the correct height.

You should fit a bell to your cycle.

You **MUST**

- ensure your brakes are efficient
- have white front and red rear lights lit when cycling at night.

Laws PCUR regs 6 & 10 & RVLR reg 18

Cycle training: if you are an inexperienced cyclist or have not ridden for a while, consider taking a cycle training course. Some councils offer national standard cycle training such as Bikeability and, in certain areas, this is free of charge. It can help build up your skills and confidence.

There are three levels to Bikeability, starting with the basics of balancing, stopping and starting safely, through to handling complex and busy junctions. You will also learn about traffic signs and the rules of the road, planning routes, safe road positioning and signalling (particularly at junctions) and basic cycle maintenance. For more information, see www.bikeability.org.uk and www.cycling.scot

2. Motorcycle licence requirements

If you have a provisional motorcycle licence, you **MUST** satisfactorily complete a compulsory basic training (CBT) course.

You can then ride unaccompanied on the public road a motorcycle up to 125 cc, with a power output not exceeding 11 kW, with L plates (in Wales either D plates or L plates, or both, can be used), for up to two years.

Law RTA 1988 sect 97(3)

To ride a moped, learners **MUST**

- be 16 or over

- have a provisional moped licence

- complete CBT training.

Law RTA 1988 sects 97(3) & 101

You can then ride unaccompanied on the public road a two-wheeled vehicle with a maximum design speed of 45 km/h (28 mph), with L plates (in Wales either D plates or L plates, or both, can be used), for up to two years.

You **MUST** first pass the theory test for motorcycles and then the moped practical test to obtain your full moped licence.

Law MV(DL)R reg 38(4)

Note. If you passed your car driving test before 1 February 2001 you are qualified to ride a moped without L plates (and/or D plates in Wales), although it is recommended that you complete CBT before riding on the road. If you passed your car driving test after this date you **MUST** complete CBT before riding a moped on the road.

Law RTA 1988 sect 97(3)

Licence categories for mopeds and motorcycles

Category AM (moped) – minimum age 16

- two-wheeled vehicle with a maximum design speed of 45 km/h (28 mph)

- three- or four-wheeled vehicle with a maximum design speed over 25 km/h (15.5 mph), up to 50 cc and with a power output not exceeding 4 kW.

Category A1 – minimum age 17

- motorcycles up to 125 cc, with a power output not exceeding 11 kW

- tricycles with a power output not exceeding 15 kW.

Category A2 – minimum age 19

- motorcycles with a power output not exceeding 35 kW.

Category A

- any motorcycle (the minimum age you can obtain a category A licence is 21 under progressive access or 24 under direct access)

- tricycles with a power output over 15 kW (minimum age 21).

Progressive access is a process that allows a rider to take a higher-category practical test if they already have at least two years' experience on a lower-category motorcycle. For example, if you have held a category A2 licence for a minimum of two years, you can take the category A practical test at age 21. There is no requirement to take another theory test.

If you want to learn to ride motorcycles larger than 125 cc and with a power output over 11 kW, you **MUST** meet the minimum age requirements, satisfactorily complete a CBT course and be accompanied by an approved instructor on another motorcycle in radio contact.

Laws MV(DL)R regs 9 & 16(7), & RTA 1988 sect 97(3)

To obtain your full moped or motorcycle licence, you **MUST** pass a motorcycle theory test and modules 1 and 2 practical tests on a two-wheeled motorcycle.

Law MV(DL)R reg 38

You **MUST NOT** carry a pillion passenger or pull a trailer until you have passed your test. Also see Rule 253 covering vehicles prohibited from motorways.

Law MV(DL)R reg 16

3. Motor vehicle documentation and learner driver requirements

Documents

Driving licence. You **MUST** have a valid driving licence for the category of motor vehicle you are driving. You **MUST** inform the Driver and Vehicle Licensing Agency (DVLA) if you change your name and/or address.

Law RTA 1988 sects 87 & 99(4)

Holders of non-European Community licences who are now resident in the UK may only drive on that licence for a maximum of 12 months from the date they become resident in this country.

To ensure continuous driving entitlement

- a British provisional licence should be obtained and a driving test(s) passed before the 12-month period elapses, or
- in the case of a driver who holds a licence from a country which has been designated in law for licence exchange purposes, the driver should exchange the licence for a British one.

MOT. Cars and motorcycles **MUST** normally pass an MOT test three years from the date of the first registration and every year after that. You **MUST NOT** drive a motor vehicle without an MOT certificate when it should have one. Exceptionally, you may drive to a pre-arranged test appointment or to a garage for repairs required for the test. Driving an unroadworthy motor vehicle may invalidate your insurance. From 20 May 2018, cars, vans, motorcycles and other light passenger vehicles manufactured or first registered over 40 years ago will be exempt from the MOT test, unless the vehicle has been substantially changed within the previous 30 years. Guidance on what counts as a substantial change can be found at www.gov.uk/historic-vehicles

If a vehicle that's currently exempt from the MOT test is substantially changed, the vehicle keeper cannot continue to claim an exemption from the MOT test.

Law RTA 1988 sects 45, 47, 49 & 53

Insurance. To use a motor vehicle on the road, you **MUST** have a valid insurance policy. This **MUST** at least cover you for injury or damage to a third party while using that motor vehicle. Before driving any motor vehicle, make sure that it has this cover for your use or that your own insurance provides adequate cover. You **MUST NOT** drive a motor vehicle without insurance. Also, be aware that even if a road traffic incident is not your fault, you may still be held liable by insurance companies.

Law RTA 1988 sect 143

Uninsured drivers can now be automatically detected by roadside cameras. Further to the penalties for uninsured driving listed in Annex 5, an offender's vehicle can now be seized by the police, taken away and crushed.

Law RTA 1988 sects 165a & 165b

The types of cover available are indicated below:

Third-party insurance – this is often the cheapest form of insurance, and is the minimum cover required by law. It covers anyone you might injure or whose property you might damage. It does not cover damage to your own motor vehicle or injury to yourself.

Third-party, Fire and Theft insurance – similar to third-party, but also covers you against your motor vehicle being stolen, or damaged by fire.

Comprehensive insurance – this is the most expensive but the best insurance. Apart from covering other persons and property against injury or damage, it also covers damage to your own motor vehicle, up to the market value of that vehicle, and personal injury to yourself.

Registration certificate. Registration certificates (also called harmonised registration certificates) are issued for all motor vehicles used on the road, describing them (make, model, etc.) and giving details of the registered keeper. You **MUST** notify the Driver and Vehicle Licensing Agency in Swansea as soon as possible when you buy or sell a motor vehicle, or if you change your name or address. The buyer and seller are responsible for completing the registration certificates. The seller is responsible for forwarding them to DVLA. The procedures are explained on the back of the registration certificates.

Law RV(R&L)R regs 21, 22, 23 & 24

Vehicle tax. Vehicle tax **MUST** be paid on all motor vehicles used or kept on public roads.

Law VERA sects 29 & 33

Statutory Off-Road Notification (SORN). This is a notification to the DVLA that a motor vehicle is not being used on the road. If you are the vehicle keeper and want to keep a motor vehicle untaxed and off the road you **MUST** declare SORN – it is an offence not to do so. The vehicle will remain SORN until you sell, tax or scrap it. If your vehicle is unused or off the road it **MUST** have either a SORN declaration or valid insurance.

Law RV(RL)R reg 26 & sched 4

Production of documents. You **MUST** be able to produce your driving licence, a valid insurance certificate and (if appropriate) a valid MOT certificate, when requested by a police officer. If you cannot do this you may be asked to take them to a police station within seven days.

Law RTA 1988 sects 164 & 165

Learner drivers

Learners driving a car **MUST** hold a valid provisional licence. They **MUST** be supervised by someone at least 21 years old who holds a full EC/EEA licence for that type of car (automatic or manual) and has held one for at least three years.

Laws MV(DL)R reg 16 & RTA 1988 sect 87

Vehicles. Any vehicle driven by a learner **MUST** display red L plates. In Wales, either red D plates, red L plates, or both, can be used. Plates **MUST** conform to legal specifications and **MUST** be clearly visible to others from in front of the vehicle and from behind. Plates should be removed or covered when not being driven by a learner (except on driving school vehicles).

Law MV(DL)R reg 16 & sched 4

You **MUST** pass the theory test (if one is required) and then a practical driving test for the category of vehicle you wish to drive before driving unaccompanied.

Law MV(DL)R reg 40

4. The road user and the law

Road traffic law

The following list can be found abbreviated throughout the Code. It is not intended to be a comprehensive guide, but a guide to some of the important points of law. For the precise wording of the law, please refer to the various Acts and Regulations (as amended) indicated in the Code. Abbreviations are listed on the following page.

Most of the provisions apply on all roads throughout Great Britain, although there are some exceptions. The definition of a road in England and Wales is 'any highway and any other road to which the public has access and includes bridges over which a road passes' (RTA 1988 sect 192(1)). In Scotland, there is a similar definition which is extended to include any way over which the public have a right of passage (R(S)A 1984 sect 151(1)).

It is important to note that references to 'road' therefore generally include footpaths, bridleways and cycle tracks, and many roadways and driveways on private land (including many car parks). In most cases, the law will apply to them and there may be additional rules for particular paths or ways. Some serious driving offences, including drink-driving offences, also apply to all public places, for example public car parks.

The reference to 'emergency area' in the Code is an 'emergency refuge area' as defined in the Motorways Traffic (England and Wales) Regulations 1982 as amended by the Motorways Traffic (England and Wales)(Amendment)(England) Regulations 2015.

Chronically Sick & Disabled Persons Act 1970	CSDPA
Environmental Protection Act 1990	EPA
Functions of Traffic Wardens Order 1970	FTWO
Greater London (General Powers) Act 1974	GL(GP)A
Highway Act 1835 or 1980 (as indicated)	HA
Horses (Protective Headgear for Young Riders) Act 1990	H(PHYR)A
Horses (Protective Headgear for Young Riders) Regulations 1992	H(PHYR)R
Motor Cycles (Eye Protectors) Regulations 1999	MC(EP)R
Motor Cycles (Protective Helmets) Regulations 1998	MC(PH)R
Motorways Traffic (England & Wales) Regulations 1982	MT(E&W)R
Motorways Traffic (England & Wales) (Amendment) Regulations 2004 or 2018 (as indicated)	MT(E&W)(A)R
Motorways Traffic (England & Wales) (Amendment) (England) Regulations 2015	MT(E&W)(A)(E)R
Motorways Traffic (Scotland) Regulations 1995	MT(S)R
Motorways Traffic (Scotland) (Amendment) Regulations 2004 or 2018 (as indicated)	MT(S)(A)R
Motor Vehicles (Driving Licences) Regulations 1999	MV(DL)R
Motor Vehicles (Variation of Speed Limits) (England & Wales) Regulations 2014	MV(VSL)(E&W)
Motor Vehicles (Wearing of Seat Belts) Regulations 1993	MV(WSB)R
Motor Vehicles (Wearing of Seat Belts) (Amendment) Regulations 2005 or 2006 (as applicable)	MV(WSB)(A)R
Motor Vehicles (Wearing of Seat Belts by Children in Front Seats) Regulations 1993	MV(WSBCFS)R
New Roads and Streetworks Act 1991	NRSWA
Pedal Cycles (Construction & Use) Regulations 1983	PCUR
Police Reform Act 2002	PRA
Private Crossings (Signs and Barriers) Regulations 1996	PC(SB)R
Prohibition of Smoking in Certain Premises (Scotland) Regulations 2006. Scottish SI 2006/No 90	TPSCP(S)R*
Public Passenger Vehicles Act 1981	PPVA
Road Safety Act 2006	RSA
Road Traffic Act 1984, 1988 or 1991 (as indicated)	RTA
Road Traffic Act 1988 (Prescribed Limit) (Scotland) Regulations 2014	PLSR
Road Traffic (New Drivers) Act 1995	RT(ND)A
Road Traffic Offenders Act 1988	RTOA
Road Traffic Regulation Act 1984	RTRA
Road Vehicles (Construction & Use) Regulations 1986	CUR
Road Vehicles (Construction and Use)(Amendment)(No 4) Regulations 2003	CUR(A)(No4)R
Road Vehicles (Display of Registration Marks) Regulations 2001	RV(DRM)R
Road Vehicles Lighting Regulations 1989	RVLR
Road Vehicles (Registration & Licensing) Regulations 2002	RV(R&L)R
Roads (Scotland) Act 1984	R(S)A
Sentencing Act 2020	SA
Smoke-free (Exemptions and Vehicles) Regulations 2007 SI 2007/765	TSf(EV)*
Smoke-free Premises etc (Wales) Regulations 2007 SI 2007/W787	TSfP(W)R*
Smoke-free Premises etc (Wales) (Amendment) Regulations 2015	S-f(W)R
Smoke-free (Private Vehicles) Regulations 2015	S-f(PV)R
Smoking Prohibition (Children in Motor Vehicles) (Scotland) Act 2016	SP(CIMV)(S)A
Traffic Management Act 2004	TMA
Traffic Signs Regulations & General Directions 2016	TSRGD
Use of Invalid Carriages on Highways Regulations 1988	UICHR
Vehicle Excise and Registration Act 1994	VERA

Acts and regulations are available as enacted or as amended at www.legislation.gov.uk and are available in their original print format from The Stationery Office as detailed inside the back cover.

* Specific legislation applies to smoking in vehicles which constitute workplaces.
For information visit: www.smokefreeengland.co.uk
www.ashscotland.org.uk/go-smoke-free www.gov.wales/smoking

5. Penalties

Parliament sets the maximum penalties for road traffic offences. The seriousness of the offence is reflected in the maximum penalty. It is for the courts to decide what sentence to impose according to circumstances.

The penalty table later in this section indicates some of the main offences, and the associated penalties. There is a wide range of other more specific offences which, for the sake of simplicity, are not shown here. The penalty points and disqualification system is described below.

Penalty points and disqualification

The penalty point system is intended to deter drivers and motorcyclists from following unsafe motoring practices. Certain non-motoring offences, eg failure to rectify vehicle defects, can also attract penalty points. The court **MUST** order points to be endorsed on the licence according to the fixed number or the range set by Parliament. The accumulation of penalty points acts as a warning to drivers and motorcyclists that they risk disqualification if further offences are committed.

Law RTOA sects 44 & 45

A driver or motorcyclist who accumulates 12 or more penalty points within a three-year period **MUST** be disqualified. This will be for a minimum period of six months, or longer if the driver or motorcyclist has previously been disqualified.

Law RTOA sect 35

For every offence which carries penalty points the court has a discretionary power to order the licence holder to be disqualified. This may be for any period the court thinks fit, but will usually be between a week and a few months.

In the case of serious offences, such as dangerous driving and drink-driving, the court **MUST** order disqualification. The minimum period is 12 months, but for repeat offenders or where the alcohol level is high, it may be longer. For example, a second drink-drive offence in the space of 10 years will result in a minimum of three years' disqualification.

Law RTOA sect 34

Penalty table

Offence	Maximum Penalties			Penalty Points
	Imprisonment	Fine	Disqualification	
*Causing death by dangerous driving	Life	Unlimited	Obligatory – 5 years minimum	3–11 (if exceptionally not disqualified)
*Dangerous driving	2 years	Unlimited	Obligatory	3–11 (if exceptionally not disqualified)
*Causing death by careless driving under the influence of drink or drugs	Life	Unlimited	Obligatory – 5 years minimum	3–11 (if exceptionally not disqualified)
Careless and inconsiderate driving	–	Unlimited	Discretionary	3–9
Driving while unfit through drink or drugs or with excess alcohol; or failing to provide a specimen for analysis	6 months	Unlimited	Obligatory	3–11 (if exceptionally not disqualified)
Failing to stop after an accident or failing to report an accident	6 months	Unlimited	Discretionary	5–10
Driving while disqualified	6 months (12 months in Scotland)	Unlimited	Discretionary	6
Driving after refusal or revocation of licence on medical grounds	6 months	Unlimited	Discretionary	3–6
Driving without insurance	–	Unlimited	Discretionary	6–8
Using a vehicle in a dangerous condition	–	LGV Unlimited PCV Unlimited other £2,500	Obligatory if offence committed within 3 years of a previous conviction for a similar offence - 6 months min. Otherwise discretionary	3 in each case
Failure to have proper control of vehicle or full view of the road and traffic ahead	–	£1,000 (£2,500 for PCV or goods vehicle)	Discretionary	3
Using a hand-held mobile phone when driving	–	£1,000 (£2,500 for PCV or goods vehicle)	Discretionary	6
Driving otherwise than in accordance with a licence	–	£1,000	Discretionary	3-6
Speeding	–	£1,000 (£2,500 for motorway offences)	Discretionary	3–6 or 3 (fixed penalty)
Traffic light offences	–	£1,000	Discretionary	3
No MOT certificate	–	£1,000	–	–
Seat belt offences	–	£500	–	–
Dangerous cycling	–	£2,500	–	–
Careless cycling	–	£1,000	–	–
Cycling on pavement	–	£500	–	–
Failing to identify driver of a vehicle	–	£1,000	Discretionary	6

* Where a court disqualifies a person on conviction for one of these offences, it must order an extended retest. The courts also have discretion to order a retest for any other offence which carries penalty points, an extended retest where disqualification is obligatory, and an ordinary test where disqualification is not obligatory.

Furthermore, in some serious cases, the court **MUST** (in addition to imposing a fixed period of disqualification) order the offender to be disqualified until they pass a driving test. In other cases the court has a discretionary power to order such disqualification. The test may be an ordinary length test or an extended test according to the nature of the offence.

Law RTOA sect 36

New drivers. Special rules as set out below apply for a period of two years from the date of passing their first driving test, to drivers and motorcyclists from

- the UK, EU/EEA, the Isle of Man, the Channel Islands or Gibraltar who passed their first driving test in any of those countries;

- other foreign countries who have to pass a UK driving test to gain a UK licence, in which case the UK driving test is treated as their first driving test; and

- other foreign countries who (without needing a test) exchanged their licence for a UK licence and subsequently passed a UK driving test to drive another type of vehicle, in which case the UK driving test is treated as their first driving test. For example a driver who exchanges a foreign licence (car) for a UK licence (car) and who later passes a test to drive another type of vehicle (eg an HGV) will be subject to the special rules.

Where a person subject to the special rules accumulates six or more penalty points before the end of the two-year period (including any points acquired before passing the test), their licence will be revoked automatically. To regain the licence they must reapply for a provisional licence and may drive only as a learner until they pass a further driving test. (Also see Annex 8 Safety code for new drivers.)

Law RT(ND)A

Note. This applies even if they pay for offences by fixed penalty. Drivers in the first group (UK, EU/EEA, etc.) who already have a full licence for one type of vehicle are not affected by the special rules if they later pass a test to drive another type of vehicle.

Other consequences of offending

Where an offence is punishable by imprisonment then the vehicle used to commit the offence may be confiscated.

Law SA sects 152, 153, 154 & 155

In addition to the penalties a court may decide to impose, the cost of insurance is likely to rise considerably following conviction for a serious driving offence. This is because insurance companies consider such drivers are more likely to be involved in a collision.

Drivers disqualified for drinking and driving twice within 10 years, or once if they are over two and a half times the legal limit, or those who refused to give a specimen, also have to satisfy the Driver and Vehicle Licensing Agency's Medical Branch that they do not have an alcohol problem and are otherwise fit to drive before their licence is returned at the end of their period of disqualification. Persistent misuse of drugs or alcohol may lead to the withdrawal of a driving licence.

6. Vehicle maintenance, safety and security

Vehicle maintenance
Take special care that lights, brakes, steering, exhaust system, seat belts, demisters, wipers, washers and any audible warning systems are all working. Also

- lights, indicators, reflectors, and number plates **MUST** be kept clean and clear
- windscreens and windows **MUST** be kept clean and free from obstructions to vision
- lights **MUST** be properly adjusted to prevent dazzling other road users. Extra attention needs to be paid to this if the vehicle is heavily loaded
- exhaust emissions **MUST NOT** exceed prescribed levels
- ensure your seat, seat belt, head restraint and mirrors are adjusted correctly before you drive
- ensure that items of luggage are securely stowed.
Laws RVLR regs 23 & 27, & CUR regs 30 & 61

Warning displays. Make sure that you understand the meaning of all warning displays on the vehicle instrument panel. Do not ignore warning signs, they could indicate a dangerous fault developing.

- When you turn the ignition key, warning lights will be illuminated but will go out when the engine starts (except the handbrake warning light). If they do not, or if they come on while you are driving, stop and investigate the problem, as you could have a serious fault.

- If the charge warning light comes on while you are driving, it may mean that the battery isn't charging. This should also be checked as soon as possible to avoid loss of power to lights and other electrical systems.

Window tints. You **MUST NOT** use a vehicle with excessively dark tinting applied to the windscreen, or to the glass in any front window to either side of the driver. Window tinting applied during manufacture complies with the Visual Light Transmittance (VLT) standards. There are no VLT limits for rear windscreens or rear passenger windows.

Laws RTA 1988 sect 42 & CUR reg 32

Tyres. Tyres **MUST** be correctly inflated to the vehicle manufacturer's specification for the load being carried. Always refer to the vehicle's handbook or data. Tyres should also be free from certain cuts and other defects.

Cars, light vans and light trailers **MUST** have a tread depth of at least 1.6 mm across the central three-quarters of the breadth of the tread and around the entire circumference.

Motorcycles, large vehicles and passenger-carrying vehicles **MUST** have a tread depth of at least 1 mm across three-quarters of the breadth of the tread and in a continuous band around the entire circumference.

Mopeds should have visible tread.

Be aware that some vehicle defects can attract penalty points.

Tyre age. Tyres over 10 years old **MUST NOT** be used on the front axles of

- goods vehicles with a maximum gross weight of more than 3.5 tonnes
- passenger vehicles with more than 8 passenger seats.

Additionally, they **MUST NOT** be used on the rear axles of passenger vehicles with 9 to 16 passenger seats, unless equipped with twin wheels.

To prove the age of a tyre, it is further required that the date of tyre manufacture marking **MUST** always be legible.

Vehicles currently excluded from tyre roadworthiness regulations and vehicles of historical interest which are not used for commercial purpose are exempt from these requirements.

Law CUR reg 27

If a tyre bursts while you are driving, try to keep control of your vehicle. Grip the steering wheel firmly and allow the vehicle to roll to a stop at the side of the road.

If you have a flat tyre, stop as soon as it is safe to do so. Only change the tyre if you can do so without putting yourself or others at risk – otherwise call a breakdown service.

Tyre pressures. Check weekly. Do this before your journey, when tyres are cold. Warm or hot tyres may give a misleading reading.

Your brakes and steering will be adversely affected by under-inflated or over-inflated tyres. Excessive or uneven tyre wear may be caused by faults in the braking or suspension systems, or wheels which are out of alignment. Have these faults corrected as soon as possible.

Fluid levels. Check the fluid levels in your vehicle at least weekly. Low brake fluid may result in brake failure and a crash. Make sure you recognise the low fluid warning lights if your vehicle has them fitted.

Before winter. Ensure that the battery is well maintained and that there are appropriate anti-freeze agents in your radiator and windscreen bottle.

Other problems. If your vehicle

- pulls to one side when braking, it is most likely to be a brake fault or incorrectly inflated tyres. Consult a garage or mechanic immediately
- continues to bounce after pushing down on the front or rear, its shock absorbers are worn. Worn shock absorbers can seriously affect the operation of a vehicle and should be replaced
- smells of anything unusual such as burning rubber, petrol or an electrical fault; investigate immediately. Do not risk a fire.

Overheated engines or fire. Most engines are water-cooled. If your engine overheats, you should wait until it has cooled naturally. Only then remove the coolant filler cap and add water or other coolant.

If your vehicle catches fire, get the occupants out of the vehicle quickly and to a safe place. Do not attempt to extinguish a fire in the engine compartment, as opening the bonnet will make the fire flare. Call the fire brigade.

Petrol stations/fuel tank/fuel leaks. Ensure that, when filling up your vehicle's tank or any fuel cans you are carrying, you do not spill fuel on the forecourt. Any spilled fuel should be immediately reported to the petrol station attendant. Diesel spillage is dangerous to other road users, particularly motorcyclists, as it will significantly reduce the level of grip between the tyres and road surface. Double-check for fuel leaks and make sure that

- you do not overfill your fuel tank
- the fuel cap is fastened securely
- the seal in the cap is not torn, perished or missing
- there is no visual damage to the cap or the fuel tank.

Emergency fuel caps, if fitted, should form a good seal.

Never smoke, or use a mobile phone, on the forecourt of petrol stations as these are major fire risks and could cause an explosion.

Undertake all aspects of the daily walkaround checks for commercial vehicles, as recommended by DVSA (www.gov.uk/dvsa/commercial-vehicle-safety) and the Fleet Operator Recognition Scheme (www.fors-online.org.uk).

Vehicle security
When you leave your vehicle you should

- remove the ignition key and engage the steering lock
- lock the car, even if you only leave it for a few minutes
- close the windows completely
- never leave children or pets in an unventilated car
- take all contents with you, or lock them in the boot. Remember, for all a thief knows a carrier bag may contain valuables
- never leave vehicle documents in the car.

For extra security fit an anti-theft device such as an alarm or immobiliser. If you are buying a new car it is a good idea to check the level of built-in security features. Consider having your registration number etched on all your car windows. This is a cheap and effective deterrent to professional thieves.

7. First aid on the road

The following information was compiled with the assistance of St John Ambulance, the British Heart Foundation and the British Red Cross. It is intended as a general guide for those without first-aid training but should not be considered a substitute for proper training. Any first aid given at the scene of an incident should be looked on only as a temporary measure until the emergency services arrive.

1. Deal with danger
Further collisions and fire are the main dangers following a crash. Approach any vehicle involved with care, watching out for spilt oil or broken glass. Switch off all engines and, if possible, warn other traffic. If you have a vehicle, switch on your hazard warning lights. Stop anyone from smoking, and put on the gloves from your first-aid kit if you have one.

2. Get help
If you can do so safely, try to get the assistance of bystanders. Get someone to call the appropriate emergency services on 999 or 112 as soon as possible. They'll need to know the exact location of the incident (including the direction of traffic, eg northbound) and the number of vehicles involved. Try to give information about the condition of any casualties, eg if anyone is having difficulty breathing, is bleeding heavily, is trapped in a vehicle or does not respond when spoken to.

3. Help those involved
DO NOT move casualties from their vehicles unless there is the threat of further danger. **DO NOT** remove a motorcyclist's helmet unless it is essential. **DO** try to keep casualties warm, dry and as comfortable as you can. **DO** give reassurance confidently and try not to leave them alone or let them wander into the path of other traffic. **DO NOT** give them anything to eat or drink.

4. Provide emergency care
Remember the letters **DR A B C:**

D – Danger Check that it is safe to approach.

R – Response Try to get a response by gently shaking the casualty's shoulders and asking loudly 'Are you all right?' If they respond, check for injuries.

If the casualty is unconscious and breathing, place them in the recovery position until medical help arrives

A – Airway If there is no response, open the casualty's airway by placing your fingers under their chin and lifting it forward.

B – Breathing Check that the casualty is breathing normally. Look for chest movements, look and listen for breathing, and feel for breath on your cheek.

If there are no signs of breathing, start CPR. Interlock your fingers, place them in the centre of the casualty's chest and press down hard and fast – around 5–6 centimetres and about twice a second. You may only need one hand for a child and shouldn't press down as far. For infants, use two fingers in the middle of the chest and press down about a third of the chest depth. Don't stop until the casualty starts breathing again or a medical professional takes over.

C – Circulation If the casualty is responsive and breathing, check for signs of bleeding. Protect yourself from exposure to blood and check for anything that may be in the wound, such as glass. Don't remove anything that's stuck in the wound. Taking care not to press on the object, build up padding on either side of the object. If nothing is embedded, apply firm pressure over the wound to stem the flow of blood. As soon as practical, fasten a pad to the wound with a bandage or length of cloth. Use the cleanest material available.

Burns. Put out any flames, taking care for your own safety. Cool the burn for at least 20 minutes with plenty of clean, cool water. Cover the burn with cling film if available. Don't try to remove anything that's sticking to the burn.

Be prepared. Always carry a first-aid kit – you might never need it, but it could save a life. Learn first aid – you can get training from a qualified organisation such as St John Ambulance, St Andrew's First Aid, British Red Cross or any suitable qualified body (see Other information for contact details).

8. Safety code for new drivers

Once you have passed the driving test you will be able to drive on your own. This will provide you with lots of opportunities but you need to remain safe. Even though you have shown you have the skills you need to drive safely, many newly qualified drivers lack experience. You need to continue to develop your skills, especially anticipating other road users' behaviour to avoid having a collision. As many as one new driver in five has some kind of collision in their first year of driving. This code provides advice to help you get through the first 12 months after passing the driving test, when you are most vulnerable, as safely as possible.

- Many of the worst collisions happen at night. Between midnight and 6 am is a time of high risk for new drivers. Avoid driving then unless it's really necessary.

- If you are driving with passengers, you are responsible for their safety. Don't let them distract you or encourage you to take risks. Tell your passengers that you need to concentrate if you are to get to your destination safely.

- Never show off or try to compete with other drivers, particularly if they are driving badly.

- Don't drive if you have consumed any alcohol or taken drugs. Even over-the-counter medicines can affect your ability to drive safely – read the label to see if they may affect your driving.

- Make sure everyone in the car is wearing a seat belt throughout the journey.

- Keep your speed down – many serious collisions happen because the driver loses control, particularly on bends.

- Most new drivers have no experience of driving high-powered or sporty cars. Unless you have learnt to drive in such a vehicle you need to get plenty of experience driving on your own before driving a more powerful car.

- Driving while uninsured is an offence. See Annex 3 for information on types of insurance cover.

REMEMBER that under the New Drivers Act you will have your licence revoked if you get six penalty points on your licence within two years of passing your first driving test. You will need to pass both the theory and practical tests again to get back your full licence.

You could consider taking further training such as Pass Plus, which could also save you money on your insurance, as well as helping you reduce your risk of being involved in a collision. There are three ways to find out more:

- internet – www.gov.uk
- telephone 0115 936 6504
- email – passplus@dvsa.gov.uk

Other information

Metric conversions

The conversions given throughout *The Highway Code* are rounded but a detailed conversion chart is shown below.

Miles	Kilometres	Miles	Kilometres
1.00	1.61	40.00	64.37
5.00	8.05	45.00	72.42
10.00	16.09	50.00	80.47
15.00	24.14	55.00	88.51
20.00	32.19	60.00	96.56
25.00	40.23	65.00	104.60
30.00	48.28	70.00	112.65
35.00	56.33		

Useful websites

GOV.UK (www.gov.uk)
St John Ambulance (www.sja.org.uk)
St Andrew's First Aid (www.firstaid.org.uk)
British Red Cross (www.redcross.org.uk)
National Highways (nationalhighways.co.uk)
Transport Scotland (www.transport.gov.scot)
Transport Wales (gov.wales/roads-driving)
Traffic England (www.trafficengland.com)
Traffic Scotland (traffic.gov.scot)
Traffic Wales (traffic.wales)
Road Safety GB (roadsafetygb.org.uk)

Ask the police: frequently asked questions database
(www.askthe.police.uk)
Traffic Penalty Tribunal (outside London)
(www.trafficpenaltytribunal.gov.uk)
London Tribunals (inside London) (www.londontribunals.gov.uk)
Traveline (www.traveline.info)
European Commission – road safety abroad
(ec.europa.eu/transport/road_safety/going_abroad/index_en.htm)
European New Car Assessment Programme
(www.euroncap.com/en)

Further reading

Best practice
Further information about good driving and riding practice can
be found in the Driver and Vehicle Standards Agency books *The
Official DVSA Guide to Driving – the essential skills* and *The Official
DVSA Guide to Riding – the essential skills*. Information specifically
for drivers of large vehicles can be found in *The Official DVSA Guide
to Driving Goods Vehicles* and *The Official DVSA Guide to Driving
Buses and Coaches*.

The Blue Badge scheme
Get information about the Blue Badge scheme from your council.

Code of practice for horse-drawn vehicles
The code of practice is available from Department for Transport,
International Vehicle Standards, Great Minster House,
33 Horseferry Road, London SW1P 4DR. Tel 0300 330 3000.
www.gov.uk/government/publications/code-of-practice-for-
horse-drawn-vehicles

Special types of vehicles
Further information about the use of special types of vehicles under
the authority of the Road Vehicles (Authorisation of Special
Types) (General) Order 2003 (STGO) or Special Orders can
be found in the Special types enforcement guide
(www.gov.uk/government/publications/special-types-
enforcement-guide/special-types-enforcement-guide).

Towing

Further information about towing safely can be found at

- Tow a trailer with a car: safety checks
  (www.gov.uk/guidance/tow-a-trailer-with-a-car-safety-checks)

- Towing a trailer with a car (www.gov.uk/towing)

- Requirements for towing trailers in Great Britain
  (www.gov.uk/government/publications/inf30-requirements-for-
  towing-trailers-in-great-britain)

Index

The numbers in black refer to the rules, which are numbered H1 to H3 and 1 to 307.

The numbers in blue refer to page numbers everywhere else.

References beginning with 'A' refer to annexes, and references beginning with 'H' refer to 'hierarchy of road users' rules.

L

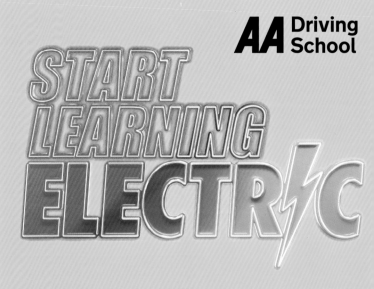

AA Driving School

START LEARNING ELECTRIC

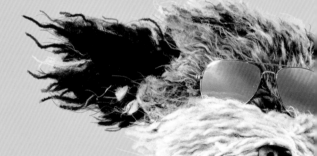

The future of driving is here.

Learn with AA Driving School.

Visit
theAA.com/driving-school

notes

Driver & Vehicle
Standards
Agency

Do you follow The Highway Code?

There are now different ways to keep up to date with The Highway Code. When you follow The Highway Code, you can

- get timely reminders and advice
- share tips with your friends and family
- always be up to date.

facebook.com/HighwayCodeGB

@ gov.uk/the-highway-code/updates

Or for tips and driving advice, follow
www.instagram.com/safe.driving.for.life